WHERE LIFE IS FOUND:

Stories of Faith, Purpose, and Belonging at Camp Barnabas

Where Life Is Found: Stories of Faith, Purpose, and Belonging at Camp Barnabas
Copyright © 2024 The Barnabas Foundation. All rights reserved.

No part of this publication may be reproduced or used in any manner without the prior written permission of the publisher, except for the use of brief quotations as in a book review.

Hardcover: 979-8-9890772-0-5
Paperback: 979-8-9890772-1-2
Ebook: 979-8-9890772-2-9

Written by Ruthie Burrell with Rooted Biography
Edited by Sara Brunsvold and Missy Bari
Cover design by Vanessa Mendozzi
Layout by Camby Designs
Cover photograph by Camp Barnabas

Interior photographs from personal collections of persons interviewed in the making of this book, Camp Barnabas, and Barnabas Prep. Used with permission.

Unless otherwise indicated, all Scripture quotations are taken from THE HOLY BIBLE, NEW INTERNATIONAL VERSION®, NIV® Copyright © 1973, 1978, 1984, 2011 by Biblica, Inc.® Used by permission. All rights reserved worldwide.

Some names and identifying details have been changed to protect the privacy of individuals, including all names of Campers and Students except in instances when permission was granted by those individuals or their families or guardians.

Rooted Biography, LLC
6300 W. 143rd St.
Overland Park, KS 66223
www.rootedbiography.com

DEDICATION

To Paul and Cyndy for their countless steps of faith to make Camp Barnabas a reality, and to every Camper and Student who has become part of the Barnabas family—you are the reason we do what we do.

TABLE OF CONTENTS

Welcome to Camp Barnabas — 11

Part 1 — 13

Chapter 1: Provision, One Piece at a Time: *Paul and Cyndy Teas, Founders* — 15

Chapter 2: Ten Thousand Things God Did: *Paul and Cyndy Teas, Founders* — 23

Chapter 3: Christ at the Center: *Peter Herschend, Board Member* — 29

Chapter 4: Find Another Way: *Sean Lewis, Camper* — 33

Chapter 5: Where God Vacations: *Mark and Paula Sterns, Cabin Dad and Nurse* — 39

Chapter 6: The Faith and Generosity of Many: *Robin Walker, Board Member* — 45

Chapter 7: The Best Place on Earth: *Jenn (Reier) Rodemeyer, Staff* — 53

Chapter 8: Enduring Reach: *Bob Speizer, Youth Pastor* — 61

Chapter 9: Unexpected Gifts: *Glenda Blevins, Nurse* — 67

Chapter 10: Continued Transformation: *Daniel Townsend, Summer Staff* — 75

Chapter 11: Perspective Shifts and Life Changes: *Mike Mrosko, Camp Director* — 83

Part 2 — 89

Chapter 12: An Extreme Opportunity to Serve: *Steve Butcher, Board Member* — 91

Chapter 13: The Joy of Welcome: *Libby Schaller, Parent* — 97

Chapter 14: The True Gift Is Your Heart: *Rhonda Francka, Camper* — 103

Chapter 15: An Invitation to Community: *Carley McGovern, Camper* — 109

Chapter 16: An Unshakable Experience: *Jake and Whitney Hornberger, Missionaries and Summer Staff* — 115

Chapter 17: Respite for the Whole Family: *Becky Korasick, Parent* — 123

Chapter 18: The Gift of Connection: *Lorie Sparks, Camper* — 131

Part 3 — 135

Chapter 19: Beautiful and Whole: *Sandy Miller, Director of Barnabas Prep* — 137

Chapter 20: A Change of Heart: *Nathan Doss, Barnabas Prep Resident Coordinator* — 145

Chapter 21: A Foundation of Love: *Millie Moyer, Barnabas Prep Resident Coordinator* — 149

Chapter 22: A Little Piece of Heaven: *Ashia Puckett, Missionary and Barnabas Prep Fellow* — 153

Chapter 23: Giving It All to God: *Jack Sadler, Barnabas Prep Fellow* — 157

Chapter 24: Positioned for a Purpose: *Bekah Walker, Barnabas Prep Fellow* — 163

Chapter 25: In Their Own Words: *Barnabas Prep Students* — 167

Part 4 — 171

Chapter 26: A God-Sized Vision: *John Tillack, CEO* — 173

Chapter 27: Walking with the Hurting: *Melissa Pardeck, Parent and Executive Assistant/Development Specialist* — 179

Chapter 28: A Profound Impact: *Don, Jennifer, Makena, and Isabella Hubbs, Parents, Sibling, and Camper* — 185

Chapter 29: Deep Joy and Heavy Responsibility: *Bernadette Losh, Executive Director of Health Services* — 191

Chapter 30: Story Builds Upon Story: *Debbie Weathermon, Parent and Development Director* — 199

Chapter 31: All Things New: *Jermaine Harrison, Youth Pastor* — 207

Chapter 32: Deeply Rooted Passion: *Caroline Tillack, Summer Staff and Development Specialist* — 215

Chapter 33: A Perfect Opportunity: *Dr. Jake Spain, Doctor* — 221

Chapter 34: Rest and Belonging: *Jenn and Tyler Moore, Parents* — 229

Afterword: Embracing the Extraordinary Journey of Barnabas — 237

Appendix: A Brief History of Camp Barnabas and Barnabas Prep — 238

Index of Terms — 240

Welcome to Camp Barnabas

Dozens of cars wind their way through narrow country roads about sixty miles southwest of Springfield, Missouri, until, one by one, they converge outside a rust-brown gate graced by a caterpillar on the left side and a butterfly on the right. Beyond the gate, dozens of teenagers and adults dressed in brightly colored T-shirts congregate, ready to welcome the caravan in. The sense of excitement is palpable.

Promptly at 4:00 p.m., the gates swing wide, and the line of cars begins to move, crossing beneath the sign welcoming them to Camp Barnabas.

The cars stream into a field just south of the gate and proceed past a series of white tents. At one tent, Campers check in. At the next, parents and guardians hand over large Ziploc bags containing their Camper's medications to a volunteer medical professional. A crowd of middle school students swoops in to take the Campers' luggage. Finally, the cars approach a tunnel of cheering teenagers.

"We love Campers, yes, we do! We love Campers—how 'bout you?" they shout, the chant bouncing from one side of the road to the other.

The Camper hops out of the car. His or her one-on-one volunteer for the week offers a wide smile in greeting.

"Bye, Mom. I'll see you later."

Then the Camper is off, moving toward the cheering crowd.

Some Campers grin and pump their fists, dashing through the tunnel and exulting in the crowd's excitement. Others duck their heads from the excessive attention. At the request of some Campers, the noise quiets, and the volunteers jump up and down in silent excitement.

Some Campers use wheelchairs. Some are missing limbs. Some are young, no more than seven or eight years old. Some are nearing fifty.

But, without fail, all are celebrated. It's a welcome many have compared to how they imagine heaven will be—a place of joy and unconditional love as Jesus welcomes His children home.

Founded by Paul and Cyndy Teas in 1994, Camp Barnabas is a Christian summer camp that seeks to change lives through disability ministry. From the beginning, Camp was designed to offer a safe, welcoming environment and accessible experiences to anyone with chronic illnesses or disabilities—from cancer and hemophilia, to cerebral palsy, Down syndrome, autism spectrum disorder, spinabifida, visual or hearing impairment, and more. Each Camper is paired with a one-on-one volunteer, called a "Missionary," who spends the week hanging out with the Camper and serving in whatever ways that Camper may need. At Camp Barnabas, differences unite rather than separate. From the activities that are open to all to the meaningfulness of connecting with others with similar experiences, every week is designed to communicate love, dignity, and value to Campers.

In 2011, the vision for Barnabas expanded to include Barnabas Prep, a Christ-centered collegiate program located near Lake Taneycomo in Branson, Missouri, that is designed to equip young adults with disabilities to achieve high levels of independence. Students spend each school year living in a dorm-like setting, building community, and taking classes in subjects like job skills, fitness, and biblical studies.

Today, nearly thirty years since Camp started, over 93,600 Campers, Students, and volunteers have found a place to belong at Barnabas, as well as a new perspective on life because of their experiences. Many now consider Barnabas a vital part of their year.

This book provides a glimpse into the ministries of Camp Barnabas and Barnabas Prep through the eyes of those who have experienced both firsthand. From Staff to volunteers, Campers to parents, these stories are a testimony to the many ways God has used a small camp in Missouri to change lives.

Philippians 2:3-11 says:

"Do nothing out of selfish ambition or vain conceit. Rather, in humility value others above yourselves, not looking to your own interests but each of you to the interests of the others. In your relationships with one another, have the same mindset as Christ Jesus: Who, being in very nature God, did not consider equality with God something to be used to his own advantage; rather, he made himself nothing by taking the very nature of a servant, being made in human likeness. And being found in appearance as a man, he humbled himself by becoming obedient to death—even death on a cross! Therefore God exalted him to the highest place and gave him the name that is above every name, that at the name of Jesus every knee should bow, in heaven and on earth and under the earth, and every tongue acknowledge that Jesus Christ is Lord, to the glory of God the Father."

In each fun activity, time of worship, and moment of connection, Camp Barnabas aims to embody the mindset of Christ. As the thousands of people who have entered through Camp's gates will tell you, encountering Jesus changes everything. This way of living and serving—in which love for others is placed above love of self—is where new life is found.

Welcome to Camp Barnabas, reader. You belong here.

Part 1

"I wouldn't have a lot of the relationships that I have today if it wasn't for Camp Barnabas. Not only is it somewhere safe [where Campers] can go for almost a week, it's also a place where they can learn about the Lord, reunite with old friends, and also make new ones."

– Steven M., Camper

CHAPTER 1

Provision, One Piece at a Time: Paul and Cyndy Teas, Founders

The vision for Camp Barnabas began with a single conversation with a young girl.

Paul and Cyndy Teas had moved from Dallas, Texas, to Branson, Missouri, in 1991 after feeling a call from God that Cyndy was meant to take a job as director of nursing at Kanakuk Kamps, a Christian summer camp for kids and teenagers.

Cyndy had served as a volunteer nurse at Kanakuk for two weeks the summer before, during which she met and bonded with a young girl named Lauren. In the summer of 1992, after Cyndy had become the director of nursing, one of the nurses told Cyndy that twelve-year-old Lauren had been coming in every day asking for ibuprofen, complaining that her leg hurt.

On the last day of camp, Cyndy made it her mission to find Lauren's mom.

"I told her I felt like she needed to have [Lauren] checked by a doctor," Cyndy recalled. "A few days later, Lauren's mom called, and she said, 'Lauren has cancer. They're going to amputate her leg tomorrow.'"

It was a devastating diagnosis for an active young girl. Lauren was afraid the camp staff wouldn't allow her to return to Kanakuk the following summer, but her mom was determined.

"They will, and you will," she told her daughter. And she was right.

One evening the next summer, Cyndy took advantage of a quiet moment while sitting on a bench with Lauren to ask her how camp was going.

"I just wish I could be with other people who understand cancer," Lauren said.

Remembering that a nearby children's hospital offered a camp for kids with cancer, Cyndy asked Lauren what she thought about that option.

"It's so lame," Lauren complained. "I want a camp like Kanakuk, but with kids with cancer."

"OK, tell me what that would look like," Cyndy said.

"And she literally told me what Barnabas should look like," Cyndy remembered. "I went home and cried to Paul and said, 'We need to do this.'"

The First Summer

As Paul and Cyndy look back now, they can see that God was at work even before they were aware of it, planting seeds for the idea that would eventually become Camp Barnabas.

In 1987, Cyndy was working at Bryan's House, an organization in Dallas that ministered to children who had AIDS or whose parents had AIDS. It was still early in the AIDS pandemic, and fear surrounding the issue ran rampant. As a result, many normal childhood activities weren't available for kids at Bryan's House, including summer camps. As parents of children who had enjoyed camp, Cyndy and Paul wished the kids at Bryan's House had the chance to go too.

"[We thought] there should be a camp for kids like them. Somebody should do that," Paul remembered. "Not us, you know, but it's a good idea, and somebody needs to take that ball and run with it."

After Cyndy's conversation with Lauren, Paul and Cyndy agreed—starting this camp was something God was calling them to do. So Paul talked to Joe White, the CEO of Kanakuk Kamps, and Joe agreed to let Paul and Cyndy host an extra week of camp at the end of the summer of 1994 for kids with cancer and blood diseases.

As plans took shape, Paul and Cyndy began considering names for their camp. The perfect suggestion came from their young daughter, Kayman, who had won the Barnabas Award at Kanakuk for being an encouragement to her cabin mates. In the book of Acts, Barnabas lived up to his name—meaning "son of encouragement"—when he "encouraged [the believers in Antioch] to remain true to the Lord with all their hearts" (Acts 11:23).

"You said the purpose of camp was to encourage kids who are sick that they can do the same things others can do, so why don't you call it Camp Barnabas?" Kayman said.

The name seemed to fit, so they began to refer to their first week of camp as Kanakuk Barnabas-One, or KB-1.

Most of the campers that first year came from Oklahoma Children's Hospital, but then a woman from St. Louis heard about what the Teas family was doing and asked if she could bring her son and several of his friends who had hemophilia. Cyndy told her they were welcome to attend.

"So it ended up, with no money and no budget to market or anything, we had thirty-five campers that first summer," Cyndy said. "That was the first year that we did the program, and it just really blessed us. So we started dreaming: 'What if we could have a whole camp that did this all summer for different disease types or different disabilities?'"

Around this same time, Jim Behling, Cyndy's boss at Kanakuk and a good friend of the Teas family, asked Cyndy what she hoped to do with the program moving forward. She described to him the dreams she and Paul had of opening a full camp tailored to children with needs that traditional camps may not be able to support.

He listened thoughtfully and then said, "I know a camp that's for sale."

Cyndy still remembers the moment as though it were yesterday. The 100-plus-acre campground was located near Purdy, Missouri, about an hour southwest of Springfield.

"Well, that's great, but I don't have any money," she replied. "It takes money to buy a camp."

"God owns all the cattle on all the hills," Jim replied. "So I think you should trust Him with it."

Jim was right: God would bring Paul and Cyndy the funds they needed at just the right time—in ways neither of them could have anticipated.

Learning from Others

"It's kind of good when you're doing something like this that you have no idea of what you're doing," Paul said. "Being ignorant is a real blessing. You know not everything's going to work, but if you hit a stumble here—well, then let's try this. But it's just because you don't know any better, so you keep going forward with it.

"God was just unbelievably generous and patient. I'm sure we gave Him a lot of gray hairs, but things just came together, and we always met the right person at the right time that opened the next door and let us keep moving forward with this deal."

One example of God opening a door had its beginnings in the early 1990s when Cyndy was still working at Kanakuk. While visiting her sister in Dallas, Cyndy found an issue of the *Parade* Sunday newspaper magazine on her bedside table.

"Why is this magazine in here?" Cyndy asked.

Paul and Cyndy Teas, Founders of Camp Barnabas

"Oh, there's a cool story about a camp for people with disabilities," her sister said. "I thought you'd like it."

Cyndy hadn't told her sister about their plans for a camp yet, and she couldn't believe the irony. She read the article and realized the featured camp, Camp John Mark, wasn't very far from Dallas, so she talked her sister into going with her to visit. The camp wasn't in session, but Cyndy loved its mission and was impressed by its facilities. Though it wasn't a Christian camp, the director was a Christian, and Cyndy remembers how helpful and encouraging he was when he learned she was considering starting a similar camp.

"He didn't at all go, 'Are you out of your mind? What do you think you're doing, girl?'" Cyndy said. "[Now] I just think, 'What if that's just another piece of how God worked?' That silly little magazine that comes with the newspaper, and my sister's like, 'Oh, you need to see this,' just because I worked at a camp, not at all thinking I had an idea to do something like that."

Later on, a woman who had helped Camp John Mark with some of its early fundraising and donor relations initiatives—referred to as "development" in the nonprofit world—came to work as a nurse for Cyndy at Kanakuk.

"I shared that we had done this week for kids with cancer, and we were hoping to do something [bigger] someday. The next thing you know, she sends me cardboard boxes, that she paid the postage on, full of all the information on how they raised the funds to get Camp John Mark going. So I was like, 'How random is that?' I mean, she was from Chattanooga, Tennessee, or something, and what made me even think to mention that to her? But I mentioned it, and it all started happening."

That same woman introduced Paul and Cyndy to a development expert named Bill Wilson.

After Paul and Cyndy shared their story with him, he said, "I'm sorry, but I can't help you. You don't have any money, and you don't have a donor base. I can't help you."

"He thought we were two crazy people," Cyndy remembered with a laugh.

Then three months later, Bill called them back.

"God won't leave me alone," he said. "I'm going to help you."

"And he helped us write a development plan. I don't think he even charged us," Cyndy said. "It was just so neat how God put another piece of the pie in place for us."

Purchasing the Property

As Paul and Cyndy were planning to host Kanakuk Barnabas-Two, their second one-week camp after the regular Kanakuk season, a man named Buddy Harper called and said he wanted to bring his entire family to volunteer with them.

"I'm really kind of full on volunteers," Cyndy told him.

"No, I want to come," Buddy insisted and went on to describe how he wanted his children to understand that other children had things to deal with that were way bigger than their issues.

Cyndy gave in, and Buddy brought his family to serve that summer.

"Where does this go from here?" Buddy asked Paul during a conversation in a free moment.

By this point, Paul and Cyndy had toured Camp Soaring Hawk, the camp Jim Behling had told them about, and Paul spent a month working there to learn how it operated. Surrounded by trees, the camp sat on a bluff overlooking a beautiful valley. The property was full of possibilities, but Paul and Cyndy still weren't sure how the financial side of things would work out.

Paul told Buddy about the camp and that he and Cyndy were starting a nonprofit and trying to raise money to purchase the property. The conversation concluded, and Paul thought nothing more of it. Not long after camp ended, though, Buddy called Paul and Cyndy's home.

Paul taking part in a Cross Carry for a Camper who passed away

"This is in the old days," Cyndy explained. "[Buddy] says, 'Go get on the other extension, Cyndy.' Paul's on one extension in one end of our house, and I'm on the other extension. And he says, 'OK, well, I went and looked at your camp,' and oh my gosh, my heart sank. I thought, 'He's gonna buy our camp. He's gonna buy it and start his own program, and we won't get to have it.' I was freaking out, which is so weird, because we had no way to buy it."

Instead, Buddy said, "I talked with the owner, and I think I got it worked out with him." He went on to explain the financial plan he'd worked out that would allow Paul and Cyndy to buy the camp.

"'Oh my gosh—what is this, God? How did this happen?'" Cyndy remembered thinking. "So Paul and I get off the phone, and we're just staring into space going, 'OK, God is really big.'"

A Perfectly Timed Donation

From there, Paul and Cyndy put together a group of board members and started their 501(c)(3). Since they still had next to no money to fund Camp Barnabas, Paul explained his and Cyndy's Plan A to the board: spend the summer of 1996 raising money and awareness and recruiting Campers, Staff, and volunteers for the next summer.

"The board goes, 'Oh no, people give to a real entity—they don't give to the idea. So you go do Camp,'" Cyndy said. "And we're like, 'OK, but our bank account has no money.'"

Paul Teas with a Camper

 The board assured Paul and Cyndy they would make sure Camp was funded, but at that point, none of them contributed anything.
 "They wanted to know that Paul and I were going to earn it, that we were going to make sure it worked and trust God with it," Cyndy said. "And it worked."
 Paul and Cyndy moved forward with hiring Staff and recruiting volunteers and launched Camp Barnabas's first summer session only six months after that conversation with the board.
 As the summer got underway, Paul and Cyndy still didn't have enough money to pay the Staff. Their first payroll was fast approaching, and Cyndy was stressed to the max. She kept asking Paul to go and talk to one of the board members who they knew would be willing to help out.
 "I'm going to," Paul reassured her, "but I'm busy running Camp. Don't worry—God has assured me we're gonna have it."
 The next day, that same board member drove up to Camp. It was a day off for their Staff, so Camp was quiet. The board member told Paul and Cyndy that he'd just received a check from a client during a meeting and wanted to give it to them.
 "It was payroll, plus $500. And he had no idea that we were about to ask him for payroll." Cyndy chuckled. "It was just such a God story. It's like, 'OK, you know what? I'm not gonna stress. God is taking care of this place.' And never in our wildest imagination would it be where it is today."
 The journey ahead was still long, but those early stories of God's provision proved to Paul and Cyndy that they were right where God wanted them to be.

"The [willingness] of Paul and Cyndy to just basically step out in faith—they saw this need and they responded—has been really inspirational to me. They didn't have all the questions answered . . . they didn't have any money. They didn't have anything. They just decided to do it. At the end of the day, if it hadn't been for them . . . and faith, [Camp Barnabas] wouldn't have happened."

– Myron M., Board Member

CHAPTER 2

Ten Thousand Things God Did:
Paul and Cyndy Teas, Founders

Looking at Camp Barnabas today, with its well-kept grounds, paved roads for wheelchairs, and beautiful air-conditioned cabins, few would guess where it started. But in the early years, it was almost like living on the frontier.

"You're having to make do and figure out how to use things," Paul Teas said. "But it all worked. [And it] pulled the Staff together, because we were all in the same boat, and it was a leaky lifeboat. Everybody's bailing like mad, but we kept sailing along."

When Paul and Cyndy returned to Camp Barnabas for its 25th anniversary in 2019, they joked with the Staff that they were spoiled.

"Because they have air conditioning, and we didn't even have asphalt for the wheelchairs to ride on." Cyndy laughed.

But they wouldn't trade the camaraderie with their Staff during those tough early years for anything. Paul and Cyndy continue to stay in touch with many of their original team members, and many of them, in turn, stay in touch with each other.

"I think that hard work of trying to make the best parties and the best activities on a budget that was just nonexistent . . . made them depend on God and each other," Cyndy said. "It put roots in their friendships, and I love that."

One of the interesting things about Camp Barnabas though, Paul said, is that "nobody does anything."

"You meet parents, and they go, 'What have you done with my child? . . . They've never had such a great attitude. They're so happy.' And I'd say, 'Well, I didn't do anything. It was their [Cabin Staff].' And you go talk to the [Cabin Staff]: 'What did you do with this Camper?' 'I didn't do anything. It was the CIA [Christian in Action, or one-on-one volunteer]. . . . And then you go talk to the CIA and go, 'What did you do?' [And they say], 'I didn't do anything. The Camper taught me so much about life and our relationship with God.'"

Paul laughed. "So essentially, nobody ever did anything at Camp. That's just how it [worked]."

"We learned very quickly that the people who work with those children—the volunteers, the Staff—they're blessed as much or more, and they're changed as much or more [than the Campers]," Cyndy said.

Maintaining Faith and a Good Attitude

Paul and Cyndy have dozens of stories about the challenges and funny things that happened in the first few years. Sometimes, God used even tough situations for the ultimate benefit of Camp.

While Paul and Cyndy were working to get Camp Barnabas off the ground, they agreed to volunteer at a youth retreat in Dallas as a favor to an old friend. They ended up with more of a challenge than they bargained for when the weather dropped from 70 degrees to 30 degrees almost overnight.

"None of us even had coats . . . and we're sleeping in tents," Cyndy said. "It was really, really hard. There was this cute young couple who was working [at the retreat], and they said, 'Hey, why don't we all get in the same tent? We can keep each other warmer.' And we're like, 'We're in. We're freezing.'"

As the four of them huddled together for warmth, the young couple, whose names were Wade and Cindy Moses, shared a little of their story, and Paul and Cyndy, in turn, shared how they were starting a Camp for kids with disabilities. They all made it through the night, a little colder for the wear, and Paul and Cyndy returned home. Not long after that, Wade and Cindy gave them a call.

"We want to work for you," they said.

Paul and Cyndy protested, emphasizing the fact that they didn't have any money to pay them, but Wade and Cindy wouldn't take no for an answer. They agreed to work without salary in exchange for a free place to live at Camp and meals from the dining hall while Camp was in session.

"It was just so funny how God put them in our path at this crazy event we went to, and they were our camp directors the first three years," Cyndy said. "Great people. We still have kept up with them."

Camp's extremely tight budget also meant that the Staff tried to fix maintenance issues themselves whenever possible. Cyndy remembered one instance where Paul and a couple male Staff Members spent all night digging holes to clear out a clog in the sewer line.

"They were up all night digging lots of holes, and I just remember Paul came in, and he said, 'Well, we found it. We found the worst part. We got it fixed. Everything's fine.' He didn't gripe or moan. He was just like, 'You know, we kind of had fun. We were just bunch of guys down digging in the dirt and the mud and the sludge.'"

Through all of those tough early years, Cyndy credits Paul's faith and good attitude with helping keep Camp going.

"I can tell you there were two or three times where I said, 'It's not working. Let's just close the gate and sell the property. . . . Let's just tell the board it's over. We can't make it work.' And Paul's like, 'Well, I tell you what, when I hear God saying that, I'll do it, but I'm not doing it with you saying it.' And he kept Camp going, just with his faith. My faith wasn't as strong, and I was ready to just hang it up. I couldn't imagine doing that, but I couldn't imagine how we were going to ever make it work. But Paul always said, 'No, it'll work. It's working. It might not be working great, but it's working.'"

Generous Blessings

For a long time, Camp Barnabas was funded by twenty-five- and fifty-dollar donations from hardworking locals who, like Camp itself, were doing their best to make ends meet.

"That was what kept us afloat," Cyndy said. "To me, that was so humbling. By the time we left, we cultivated some big donors, but the real bread-and-butter donors were what blessed me because I knew it was a sacrifice."

Over time, bigger connections began to come along as well. First was Jack Henry, founder of the financial technology company Jack Henry based in Monett, Missouri, who owned the land next to Camp Barnabas. Paul reached out to Jack when Camp needed to do some renovations near Jack's property line.

"I wanted to ask permission [since we were] gonna go stomping all over his pasture," Paul said. "He could not have been nicer. 'What are you doing?' he asked. 'And how's your funding going?' I said, 'Well, we've hit a little bit of a stumble, but you know, we'll get around it. But that's not why I'm calling,' and the conversation goes on and on. And Jack finally said, 'Well, you know, how much money are you out now?' So I gave him this figure. So he says, 'OK, I'll bring you a check.' I mean, it's like that." Paul snapped his fingers. "You know, you're just stupefied by their generosity."

Jack continued to be a good friend and supporter of Camp for many years.

Then, there was the day that Paul and Cyndy received a voicemail message from NFL player Kurt Warner.

"I'm a football player for the Rams, and I need a favorite charity," Kurt said in his message.

Paul and Cyndy's son, Trace, immediately knew Kurt's name and told them he was a new quarterback for the St. Louis Rams. The next day, Paul and Cyndy drove to St. Louis to meet with Kurt and his wife, Brenda. The Warners' son was blind, and they had heard about Camp Barnabas from their son's piano teacher who had volunteered at Camp in the past.

"That started a relationship with Kurt Warner, and the next year, he was the MVP of the Super Bowl," Cyndy said.

The next summer, the Warners' son attended Camp, their daughter participated in the Sibling Program (a program that invites siblings of children with disabilities the opportunity to attend Camp as well), and Brenda volunteered as a nurse.

Kurt's friendship, advocacy, and financial support were a huge blessing to Camp over the years.

"That was another one of those great God moments," Cyndy said.

Growth in Impact

In addition to individual donors, many people helped Camp Barnabas grow by finding creative ways to contribute to its mission. In 1999 a group called Youth Specialties offered to make Camp Barnabas a free marketing video to recruit volunteers.

Paul and Cyndy watched the video with Wade and Cindy Moses, and all four were crying by the end.

"It was the best video we ever had made," Cyndy said. "And it was free."

A few months later, the video was shown at a conference for youth leaders in Nashville, Tennessee.

"That was back in the day of pay phones. They said you couldn't get to a pay phone fast enough with all the youth leaders running out after they saw the video. 'I want to sign up my youth group. How many kids can I bring? What age group? How much does it cost?'" Cyndy smiled. "We never had to recruit volunteers after that. They came to us, which was incredible."

Then, in a huge surprise, the Teas family and Camp Barnabas were chosen in 2005 to be part of *Extreme Makeover: Home Edition*.

"It was a surprise," Paul said. "Don't play poker with those people."

"You aren't kidding," Cyndy said. "They had bamboozled us. . . . They had us convinced there's a good chance you're not going to be selected."

But Camp Barnabas was chosen, and the *Extreme Makeover* episode helped introduce Camp to many new Campers and families—and deeply impacted the show's cast and crew. In less than a week, the team completely rebuilt Paul and Cyndy's home at Camp and designed and built an indoor game space for Campers and a bunkhouse for volunteers.

Though Paul and Cyndy weren't allowed to be at Camp while the team worked on their house, they heard stories later about how more and more people from the show started wandering over to the dining hall to spend time with the Campers during Wrap Up, a Camp-wide gathering at the end of each day. By the end of the week, a couple people had become a crowd.

Two men who worked for the show separately told Paul and Cyndy that, after they finished this episode, they planned to resign and spend more time with their families, because being at Camp had reminded them of what was most important.

"It wasn't anything like they had done before," Paul said. "You know, they go in and do these projects in different towns and do some wonderful things. But then they packed up, moved on, and did the next one. But this one was different; this one stuck. And it . . . just reached them on a much more emotional level."

Many of the show's cast members were impacted too.

"The stars were genuine and kind and loving, and they fell in love with Barnabas," Cyndy said. "[Two of them] came back two different summers and just hung out with Campers for a couple of days."

Even *Extreme Makeover's* host, Ty Pennington, was deeply moved by his time at Camp Barnabas. Cyndy remembers sitting beside Paul on the final reveal day, listening while Paul chatted with Ty before taping began.

"What is it that's different about this place?" Ty asked.

"Well, it's God," Paul said and went on to describe how all the Staff and Campers knew God was working through Camp.

"About that time the director goes, 'OK, we're ready to roll,' to start filming again," Cyndy said. "Ty goes, 'I'll be right back.' And he turns around and walks to the bathroom, and he's got tears just flowing down his face. So it impacted him in a way that we'll never know."

No Regrets

For the first three years of Camp Barnabas, Paul and Cyndy didn't take salaries. Instead, they lived off their savings, and then Paul started substitute teaching in Monett while Cyndy worked for a pediatric urgent care center in Springfield.

"We knew we just couldn't take the money to pay salaries for ourselves. We had to keep the money in Barnabas," Cyndy explained. "But we look back on that time, and I don't regret that we did that. I mean, it was hard. We still had our two kids at home. They had needs, but they would tell you easily, 'I never did without. God always provided what we needed and what we wanted.' And He did, you know. . . . It was a God story every time, and it grows your faith."

Paul's only regret is that he didn't keep a log of the 10,000 things God did to keep Camp going.

"We literally started out with a blank piece of paper on the kitchen table. That's how Barnabas started. You're trying to do all these things and figure all these things out, and you would hit a point with a problem that you did not have the solution [to]. So you just stop and go, 'OK, God, you fix it,'" Paul explained. "Every time, you met somebody, you read something, you heard something—whatever it was, that was the solution to that problem. Over and over and over. If we would get out of the way and let God do what God does—and He's pretty good at what He does—things worked out."

He smiled. "That's why we say God was in the middle of it. He was up to His elbows in it. It would not have happened had not God been there."

Looking back, Cyndy is glad God only showed her part of the vision for Camp Barnabas at the beginning of things.

"If He'd shown me the whole big picture, I'd have run the other direction, because I would have known I couldn't do it, even with Him, you know? But He gave me just the vision of: 'The children with disabilities and diseases need to hear My message. You need to give it to them, and you need to do it in a fun way.'"

That compelling vision paired with God's faithfulness gave Paul and Cyndy the courage to keep moving forward with building Camp Barnabas, one small step at a time.

> *"Camp Barnabas is the closest I've come to experiencing 'Thy will be done on earth as it is in heaven.' We say those words together every Sunday morning at my church, so for our students to have a hands-on experience of what that looks like is indescribable."*
>
> *– Ashley S., Cabin Parent*

CHAPTER 3

Christ at the Center:
Peter Herschend, Board Member

Peter Herschend's involvement with Camp Barnabas was born out of friendship. In 1992, he and his first wife, JoDee, were attending Shepherd of the Hills Episcopal Church in Branson, Missouri, where they became friends with Paul and Cyndy Teas. At the time, Cyndy was working at Kanakuk Kamps as a nurse, and Paul was doing maintenance there.

"We were good friends," Peter said. "And oftentimes in coffee conversations after church . . . the four of us would talk about camp."

Peter vividly remembers the tears in Cyndy's eyes as she told them one Sunday about a young girl she'd met through Kanakuk who was going to lose part of her leg due to cancer. He also remembers the coffee meeting a little over a year later when Paul and Cyndy told them about their desire to create a camp for kids who were not able to attend traditional camps, whether due to illness or disability.

"We have to do something," they told Peter and JoDee.

Peter and JoDee had front row seats to the journey that Paul and Cyndy took from there, as they began organizing the ministry and found a property they wanted to purchase.

"They acquired Camp Soaring Hawk and put a note down [on it]," Peter said. "I can promise you, they had no idea how that note was going to get paid off. They were working on faith . . . that alone strengthened my faith in them and the Lord."

A Place for Kids to Be Kids

Paul and Cyndy asked Peter, who is one of the founders and owners of Branson's famous Silver Dollar City theme park, to be on the board for Barnabas and lend some of his business experience to the fledgling ministry.

"Course I said yes."

Peter has been on the board ever since. Throughout his years of involvement, many Campers have touched his heart, but a few stories rise to the surface.

One came early in Camp Barnabas's history.

"I clearly, clearly remember walking behind two teenage gals, both Campers. They weren't paying attention to me, and I was certainly not eavesdropping, but the wonder of Camp came through to me in this as they were just chatting back and forth."

The first girl asked the second, "What kind of cancer do you have?"

The second answered her, and the first exclaimed, "That's the same thing I have!"

Reflecting on that conversation, Peter is struck by the understanding that only comes from shared experience. In his own case, he recently had a knee replacement. While he could explain to anyone what the experience was like, only those who have been through it themselves really understand. The same was true for those two Campers.

"That is the heart of those kids being kids. It's just wonderful. 'I understand exactly what you're going through,'" he said. "That level of companionship, you can only find on a one-to-one level. . . . For those two girls, the relationship at that moment changed their lives. You don't get to see that very often."

Another story still fills him with emotion. Peter remembers watching Billy, a young Camper who was blind, learn how to shoot a rifle.

"Most people would say, 'Rifle range. Blind. Scratch that. Answer is: heck no.' But why shouldn't Billy have the experience of pulling the trigger on a rifle?"

Billy's Counselor stood right behind him, helping aim the rifle and coaching Billy through what to do.

"This is called the trigger guard," the Counselor said. "Feel it? And that's the trigger. I'll tell you when to pull it. First, we've got to finish aiming. There's a target out there, about fifty feet out. We want to hit it. I'll aim the rifle for us, but you're gonna fire it."

They finished that process, and then the Counselor told Billy to pull the trigger.

BAM.

Turning to his Counselor, Billy asked, "Did we do good?"

They did.

The moment was simple, but it touched Peter deeply. "You can't get that anywhere else but at Camp Barnabas."

One additional story involved a Camper who was blind and had some other physical challenges as well. Peter watched as she approached the high ropes course and listened to Staff Members describe the course to her.

"Do you want to try it?" they asked her.

"I'm going to be scared," she said in a halting voice.

But after some reassurance, she agreed, and they buckled her in.

"Nothing was going to happen to her," Peter said. "She was buckled in everywhere from Thursday. . . . [But] she can't see. She doesn't know where the heck she is—could be two hundred feet in the air or she could be two feet in the air. They've described to her what's going on and get her over to the end. She makes it. [Everyone's] cheering, excited, and they bring her back down in her chair. She said, 'I was so scared, but I did it.'"

He smiled. "Those are classic Barnabas stories to me."

Leading with Love

Peter has witnessed the impact of Barnabas in many ways over the years. Like many other people, he was surprised to realize that those who were perhaps most impacted by Camp weren't the Campers but the Missionaries, the one-on-one Counselors who are assigned to a specific Camper each week.

"I have a nephew who lives in Atlanta, and he was there as a Missionary for I think two, maybe three summers, at the most. He talks about it today. He's forty-five to fifty years old, and he talks about it today, how it really impacted him."

Peter has seen Camp's impact trickle down into the way he runs his business too. In particular, his experiences with Barnabas caused him to advocate for Silver Dollar City to comply with the ADA (Americans with Disabilities Act), which outlines the requirements for a facility to be accessible to people with disabilities.

"I know that my time with Barnabas impacted our ADA compliance here [at Silver Dollar City]. This is hilly country . . . it is not exactly level," he said. "I think [Barnabas] just lifted . . . our awareness of what has to be. We are ADA compliant today to the very, very best of our ability, but that has roots clear back in Camp Barnabas."

As a company, Silver Dollar City seeks to be a great place for people to work, to use sound financial principles, and, most importantly, to keep Christ at the heart of all they do.

"What's important is that we are a Christian company. We're not a church . . . . Churches have a job, and other ministries have their jobs. But our job is to be a place where you can bring your family, your kids, your grandkids, and know that you're OK. Know that it's a place that you're loved. Our basic statement is we 'Lead with love' in our company. I'm proud of that. That has worked well."

Peter sees that principle of keeping Christ and His love at the heart of everything as the key to Barnabas's success as well. He compared what happens at Barnabas to other camps that focus on crafts, sports, or other social activities. While those camps have their place and offer valuable experiences, he wondered if there is quite the same *need* for Christ-centeredness as there is at Camp Barnabas.

"Christ is at the heart of everything that Barnabas does. The leadership there is Christ-centered, and the [doctors who] come in are Christ-centered. If you weren't Christ-centered when you came in, you're probably going to be when you go away."

He recalled a story he heard of a Missionary and Camper from Barnabas who built a campfire one night and laid on their backs talking.

"They're lying flat on their backs looking up at the starry sky, and the [Missionary] brought that child to Jesus [amid the] stars and the campfire.

"Could that happen at other camps? Of course it can, and I'm sure it does," he said with a nod. "But I know it happens at Barnabas."

"Camp has changed my life forever. It has allowed me to see not only myself but people around me in a different/better light. It has taught me what it means to be unapologetically me."

– Hailey C., Missionary

CHAPTER 4

Find Another Way:
Sean Lewis, Camper

From the time Sean Lewis was young, his mom encouraged him: "You can do anything you want to do—you might just have to find another way to do it." It's a motto Sean has taken to heart.

Born with cerebral palsy, Sean has used an electric wheelchair since age six. But he has refused to let cerebral palsy define him. He earned an associate degree in human services and applied sciences. He is a motivational speaker, life coach, and advocate for people with disabilities. He has played bocce ball at the national level and dreams of representing the U.S. in the Paralympics one day. He also participates in 5Ks, 10Ks, half marathons, full marathons, and 100 milers with the assistance of a racing wheelchair and a team of people. One day he hopes to complete an Ironman Triathlon.

"For me, my joy and my strength comes from, number one, my relationship with God, but also my mom and the incredible friends that God has surround-

Sean with Paul Teas

ed me with," Sean said. "He's given me the opportunity to have an incredibly awesome life. He's used me to make an impact, to hopefully make people turn toward Him, but also to realize that, no matter what our challenges are, we can find another way."

He sees this as something Camp Barnabas does well.

"They never told anyone, 'You can't do this. You can't do that.' What they did is they adapted the equipment—they adapted whatever they had to do. They got the support to help the Campers do whatever they wanted to do."

Sean first attended Camp Barnabas in 1996 at age thirteen. Before then, although his mom had helped him find ways to be involved in plenty of activities, Sean had never experienced summer camp. During his first week at Camp, he loved getting to ride a horse, go swimming, and try new things like riflery and archery.

He also made new friends and has continued to stay in touch with many of them, even more than fifteen years later.

"Because of the environment and everything like that, you got really close to people, really fast, so you felt like family pretty quickly," he said. "Even though you hadn't known someone very long, you felt like you'd known them all your life."

Sean remains grateful for the ways Camp Barnabas helped him grow in his independence.

"Camp Barnabas was the first place I got to go for an extended amount of time away from my family, and it gave me some independence, let me know that I would be OK, that all my needs would be met and be taken care of," he said. "When my mom came to pick me up, I was already talking about what a great time I had, and I was ready to come back."

An Example for Others

As Sean grew older, he wanted to find a way to give back to Camp. He joined the MP (Missionary Partner) Program, through which he helped fill in the gaps in whatever needed to be done around Camp and talked through various issues with Missionaries about what their Camper might need. In 2006 and 2007, his last two years at Camp, he served as the Staff Minister, acting as an encourager and support to both other Staff and to Campers.

"I could be that listening ear. I could be that one to encourage them, and I helped to pick them up and keep them going," he explained. "I was also able to be an example for the other Campers and be someone they could talk to, someone who dealt with some of the same challenges they did, someone they could share with and say, 'Sean, what did you do about this? How did you go through this? Or what do you think about this?'"

He recalled one eight-year-old boy who came up to him and asked Sean how he was able to dance even while in a wheelchair. Sean was happy to explain, and then he hung out and danced with the Camper that night during the Wrap Up party.

Sean at Camp Barnabas

"That next day, his Staff found me, and [the Camper] wanted to give his heart to God. He wanted to get saved. So I got the opportunity to share Christ with him and lead him into a relationship with Christ. That was really awesome."

Another time, after Sean shared a devotional thought at Wrap Up, a Camper came up to him with tears on her cheeks.

"I want you to know, seeing you and hearing you speak lets me know that there's hope for people with disabilities," she said.

"I think God really used me to impact a lot of people, because when they saw me, they could obviously see that I had challenges," Sean said. "But I was still happy. I was still praising God. I still enjoy my life. So hopefully I was able to be an example of [how] even though you have challenges, that doesn't mean that your life sucks. Life can still be awesome—you've just got to find a different way to do the things you want to do."

Speaking Up for Change

That desire to encourage and impact others was with Sean from a very young age. At fifteen, he knew God was calling him to be a speaker. Originally, he thought that might mean going into youth ministry, but when he was in college, the call clarified into something else.

"I very quickly realized that God wanted me to take my story and my message outside the four walls of the church."

Getting his degree wasn't easy, but with some creativity and help from his mom, Sean was able to persevere.

"I have some learning challenges. I don't read or write," Sean said. "Anytime I had a book report, or I had to study for a test, my mom read it to me. [She] would stay up for hours with me, while I dictated what I wanted to say to her in a paper. Anytime I had to take a test, I had someone who would read me the questions, and then I would tell them what to write, and they wrote down exactly what I said."

Today, Sean has spoken at colleges, churches, schools, community organizations, and in the capitol building in his home state of Oklahoma. He has participated in and joined the leadership teams for multiple advocacy groups for people with disabilities, including Civitan International, The Arc of Oklahoma, and Oklahoma People First.

"I started getting more involved in advocacy because I realized I could be a voice," Sean said. "I could help make changes, and I could speak up for the people who need those changes but couldn't speak for themselves."

He's also gotten involved with a biking and pedestrian advocacy group in his hometown that helps advocate for ADA compliance.

"Even though the ADA was passed in 1995 . . . about 96 percent of all businesses you go into are not wheelchair accessible," Sean said. "I would hear from local businesses that would say, 'Well, we're not wheelchair accessible because we've never seen anybody in a chair here but you.' So it's a catch-22. They don't make the changes they need to make because they've never seen anyone in a wheelchair come into their businesses. But people with disabilities don't come in because they know it's not accessible."

Sean has found that the best way to advocate is just to live his life and let his friends and community witness some of the challenges for themselves. Many times, as he has gone about his everyday activities with friends, they have noticed the problems with accessibility and become more passionate about making things better.

"The more you're out there with your friends—at least in my case—my friends have seen, 'Oh, man, this needs to be better. This needs to change.' Because they see what things need to be changed, what things would make it easier [for me]. . . . I believe the best way to make those changes is to let people see you out there living your life, and then they'll come alongside you. They'll want to get behind you. They'll want to make things better."

A Matter of Perspective

Part of Sean's passion for advocacy comes from his knowledge that not everyone with disabilities has as strong of a support system as he does. During his time at Camp Barnabas, he heard from many Campers that Camp Staff and volunteers were some of the only positive voices in their lives.

"My mom instilled self-confidence in me and the belief that I could be anyone I wanted to be, do anything I wanted to do, and there was no reason why I shouldn't. So that's how I grew up. But I understand a lot of people with disabilities didn't grow up that way," Sean said. "Their life experience outside of Camp Barnabas wasn't very positive. For a lot of people, Camp Barnabas was one positive voice they looked forward to every year, because that was the one place they felt accepted."

That's part of why having a place like Camp Barnabas is so important, Sean explained. Sean is grateful to Paul and Cyndy Teas—who became good friends during his time at Camp—for being obedient to the vision God gave them.

"Camp Barnabas has done a lot of good for a lot of people . . . I personally believe that [Paul and Cyndy are] the ones who paved the way for all the different kinds of camp experiences we see now," Sean said. "I talk to others in my advocacy work, and so many of those people say they got the idea from going to

Sean (right) at Camp Barnabas

Camp Barnabas or touring Camp Barnabas or they were involved in it somehow. So [Paul and Cyndy] were the foundation, I believe, of a lot of good. God used them to mold and shape a lot of good, positive things in the world that continue to uplift and inspire and encourage a lot of people."

Most of all, he's grateful for the foundation of faith at the center of Camp Barnabas.

"God has always been . . . the main center of focus for Camp Barnabas. Paul and Cyndy wanted it to be a place where people can feel God's presence, and for me and other people I know, instantly, as soon as you drove in those gates, you just felt a difference. There was a peace, and it was just a beautiful place to experience the outdoors and experience the time with your friends and grow closer to God."

Sean says his own walk with God definitely deepened during his time at Camp. It's only through faith and the support of his family and friends that he is the person he is today and is able to share the message he's so passionate about.

"I believe that every one of us has a purpose, a dream. Additionally, I believe that we were all given gifts by God to help make the world around us a better place," Sean said. "In my opinion, God didn't cause a person's disability. But if you allow Him, He will use you right in the situation you're in . . . He will use it, He will use you, in spite of whatever circumstances you might find yourself in.

"For me, it's all a matter of perspective. We might not be able to control everything that happens to us in our life, but we can control our attitudes and our choices and the way we move through that. I think we all have challenges. Mine are more physical, you can see them, but every one of us has challenges. I think it's all about your perspective, your focus in life. I don't care what kind of challenge you have, I believe—if you look—you can find something to be happy about, something to be grateful about, something you can find joy in."

"[Camp Barnabas] means the happiest place of the summer! Getting to watch the Campers be told, 'Yes, you can do that,' instead of, 'No, you can't,' melts my heart every time."

– Sophie V., Missionary

CHAPTER 5

Where God Vacations:
Mark and Paula Sterns, Cabin Dad and Nurse

"I've always known that being a nurse was more than just working in a hospital or a clinic," Paula Sterns said. "I'm a nurse wherever I go."

That's part of why, as a labor and delivery nurse, Paula still found value in volunteering first at Kanakuk Kamps and then at Camp Barnabas. At Kanakuk, Paula became friends with Cyndy Teas and heard the story of Lauren, the young girl who inspired Paul and Cyndy Teas to start Barnabas. When Cyndy told her their plan to open a camp and asked if she would be interested in volunteering as a nurse, Paula wasn't sure what to expect, but she believed in the value of what Paul and Cyndy wanted to offer.

Paula's husband, Mark, got involved with Camp Barnabas through Paula. The first year he volunteered, he helped with maintenance around Camp.

"Then they switched me to Cabin Dad, because everything I worked on broke," Mark said with a laugh. "There's some things you're gifted at, and that's not one of them. But being a Cabin Dad was just incredible."

Paula and Mark got their young sons involved as well. Their boys were ages ten and twelve that first summer. Mark remembers the impact Camp Barnabas continued to have on their boys even after they returned home.

"We'd go to a restaurant, and they would look around and say, 'Owen couldn't come to this restaurant [because it isn't accessible],'" he said. "They were just all of a sudden aware of their surroundings and aware of what people, particularly in wheelchairs, had to deal with."

What's It Like to Be You?

The memories and lessons the Sterns learned at Camp Barnabas continue to play a role in their lives today.

As a nurse, Paula loved getting to know each Camper personally and learning about their various disabilities.

"One of our themes was, 'What's it like to be you?'" she said. "Cyndy made sure the nurses especially and the Counselors looked at the child and not the disability because they don't want to be identified as, 'I'm a diabetic. I have cerebral palsy.' 'No, I'm actually Jack,' 'I'm actually Emma,' 'I'm actually this person instead of a disability.' That was the greatest thing about Camp Barnabas is they can just come and be themselves, and they're treated just like a teenager or a kid."

When Cyndy needed a roster of the Campers who would be attending the week that Paula and Mark volunteered, Paula began putting together a master list of the Campers' names and the disabilities they had.

"I ended up writing a book during my journey there of all the different disabilities and also different syndromes, because some of them I had never heard of," she said.

Her work became a guidebook for nurses and Missionaries to help them understand each Camper's needs.

"I loved it," Paula said, "because I really wanted to know, 'What's it like to be you?'"

Though the nurses did their best to educate themselves, they never overlooked Campers' own knowledge or the methods Campers' parents used to care for them.

"Some of the kids, my goodness, they knew their bodies better than we did. So they would explain, 'This is what my mom does.' We never, ever discounted what their parents did in their care."

Though Paula had never worked in pediatrics, she learned so much from working with Cyndy Teas.

"Cyndy was such a good head nurse for all of us. She was so good at explaining to us what to do," Paula said. "Being under Cyndy, she taught me so much about pediatrics, about kids, about disabilities. She really prepared her nurses well."

Camper on high ropes course

The unique environment at Camp Barnabas also led to a number of amusing moments. Paula recalled hearing and saying sentences she'd never hear anywhere else, like, "Dylan, where'd you leave your legs?" "Oh, they're down by the pool." Or, to the boy who would take out his glass eyes and roll them around in his hands, "OK, put your eyes back in—it's time for bed."

She also recalled a hilarious anecdote her nephew shared from a summer when he was a Missionary. He woke up to a strange sound in the middle of the night and turned on the lights to find four boys with Down syndrome doing the Macarena.

"[They're] slapping their skin and everything. And he's going, '*What* are you doing? Go back to bed,'" Paula remembered. "He told them, 'If you keep doing that, you're going to have to be punished.' And they say, 'Well, what's the punishment?' 'Well, I'm gonna make you go pull grass.' 'Nooooo, we don't want to pull grass.'" She laughed.

Paula loves the way each child at Barnabas is celebrated for who they are.

"When the kids would come to Camp, they would introduce them, yell, 'This is so and so. Yayyy!' These kids have never been applauded before. You know, nobody yelled for them. That's what always touched us—they were going to be applauded as soon as they got there. They were going to be celebrated because they were there."

Tears rose in her eyes. "We cry a lot [when we talk about Barnabas], because we just loved it. It changed us. It really did."

For Paula personally, Barnabas provided a reconfirmation of her calling to be a nurse.

"There were times at Camp Barnabas that I thought, 'This is what I was created for. This is why I'm a nurse, not just to work in a hospital or in labor and delivery. But for right now, to take care of this boy or this girl.' You could just feel the Lord's presence. 'This is why I'm here.'"

Convicting Moments

For Mark, the memories that stand out the most revolve around various people he met.

Sean, who had cerebral palsy and used a wheelchair, said he wouldn't change his disability because there were people he could reach who he wouldn't be able to if he didn't use a wheelchair.[1]

Justin, who had neurofibromatosis, a condition which causes tumors, said he couldn't remember having a bad day in his life.[2]

Noah, a young Missionary, initially chose an easier Camper to care for but then felt convicted about taking the easy way out and switched to work with someone else. At the end of the week, he told Mark he'd never worked so hard or had so much fun.

---

[1] Sean's story can be read in Chapter 4.
[2] Justin's story can be read, in part, as shared by Daniel Townsend in Chapter 10.

Almost every summer they spent at Camp, Mark wrote short reports and emailed them to friends back home. In August 2005, Mark wrote, "I'm attaching a picture of thirteen-year-old Devin who was in my cabin. Devin and I went to Inspiration Point at sunset, and he was asking me about the names on the cross [of Campers who had passed away]. Devin was born blind but sees more than most people I know. He is very perceptive and loves the Lord. He knows that the first face he sees will be Jesus, and he's looking forward to it. Devin will be on the [*Extreme Makeover*] program singing 'Amazing Grace' to the workers and design team and Ty Pennington. The tears flowed when he got to the end and sang, 'Twas blind but now I see.' May the Lord use this moment to touch millions of hearts."

Mark and Paula were both at Camp Barnabas during the week that the *Extreme Makeover: Home Edition* team came. Devin's rendition of "Amazing Grace" wasn't the only touching moment of the week. Partway through the week, Mark noticed one of the cameramen watching from a distance as the Campers played in the pool.

Emotion rose as Mark remembered the conversation that followed.

"He was just amazed, because they were so natural and unashamed of their conditions—and you could see all kinds of different things that I'd never seen in terms of maladies or deformities. But he—he couldn't believe it. He said, 'You know what, I was shot in a drive-by. I grew up in Watts,' or some inner-city area of LA. He lifted up his shirt, and he had a pretty bad scar on his stomach. He said, 'I would never take my shirt off in public, and look at these kids.' So I was able to just share with him [about] the Lord, and he said, 'This week's changed my life.'"

Faith in the Middle of Hard Times

For all the beautiful and fun moments, Camp brought difficult moments too and sometimes raised tough questions. Mark remembered always crying at the beginning of the week, saddened by the severity of some of the disabilities that Campers faced. He always avoided crying around the Campers, but as the week went on, he found he didn't need to worry about avoiding that anymore, because he stopped noticing the disabilities and just enjoyed the time with the Campers.

The Cross Carry—a point in the week when Campers and Staff pause to remember friends of Camp who passed away in the last year—could be particularly hard.

"We got very attached to these kids, and they became like our kids," Paula said. "We came back to Camp each year, and we'd say, 'Hey, where's so and so?' 'Oh, they passed away this summer, and their name is [on the cross].' . . . It's like losing a child in a way."

As a nurse, seeing unhealed disabilities was also hard for Paula at times.

"It's hard for me to understand. I have scoliosis. It's not disabling, but it's bothersome. And I've prayed for healing, but it hasn't happened this side of heaven yet," she said. "It's hard to know how to pray for these kids. Do we pray

Paula with Sean Lewis

for them to be healed? If they're all healed, there won't be a Camp Barnabas—wouldn't that be great?"

She remembers one particularly impactful prayer time when she prayed for a friend in a wheelchair.

"I was saying, 'Lord, heal him,' . . . and I specifically heard the Lord say, 'Don't touch what I'm doing in his life.' And I thought, 'OK, OK.' These kids . . . they wanted to be healed. But they also had a deeper faith in following Him. . . . They still trusted in Jesus, and they still loved Him."

That emphasis on Jesus provided a central focus each week of Camp, an anchor in the midst of difficulties. Paula vividly remembers the devotions Paul Teas would share each Sunday morning at Inspiration Point, a gathering place at the edge of Camp that overlooks the valley below. Though the spiritual content was real and deep, faith talks at Barnabas never felt churchy. To Paula, it felt like a family sharing and fellowshipping together.

"There was always an emphasis on, 'Where's Jesus in the middle of this?'" Paula said. "We used to joke that [Camp Barnabas] was where God vacations. . . . [Camp Barnabas is] such a real place where His presence is so strong. Nobody is pretending; nobody is religious. It is just where you get to be the creative person that you are, and the Lord loves being there with us."

"I felt like God had driven me [to Camp] so I [could] get out of my shell again and be able to love and take care of someone I don't even know. I didn't even know that Camp Barnabas was absolutely what I needed."

– Rolando R., Missionary

CHAPTER 6

The Faith and Generosity of Many:
Robin Walker, Board Member

For Robin Walker, the story of Camp Barnabas is first and foremost one about faith and watching God work in many ways through many people. Though he has been involved with Camp from nearly the beginning, when he talks about his experiences, Robin is quick to list the people who have made an impact on Camp over the years.

Paul and Cyndy Teas, who carried the vision for Camp Barnabas and worked hard to see it fulfilled: "I'd want to give them all the credit in the world for following the vision, because it was very difficult. There was not a book on how to start a Christian camp. You just did it as God was leading you."

The Norwoods, who owned Camp Soaring Hawk, which later became Camp Barnabas: "They were able to give us some really good terms on the purchase of the property . . . without the Norwoods, Camp might have never been a physical place."

Kurt Warner, NFL quarterback and the MVP of Super Bowl 2000: "Kurt, every time they stuck a microphone in his face, would say, 'First things first, let's give glory to God,' and then second of all, 'Have you heard about my friends at Camp Barnabas?'"

Terry Winkler, who served as a board member and used a wheelchair: "[It was] really important to have him on the board, because his perception of things as a wheelchair user was so much different than ours. He was just a huge advocate for the [Campers]."

Woody Justice, a gemologist and the "best marketing person in southwest Missouri ever" who served on Camp's board for several years: "He owned a beautiful jewelry store in Springfield—his daughters still run it. He became a great friend of Camp and started a program where if you went in to have a watch battery replaced, he didn't charge for it, but he would encourage you to make a contribution to Camp Barnabas."

These are just a few examples of those who have made an impact.

"To think of where we are today, it's humbling, because there's just been a lot of input from a lot of people to get us here," Robin said. "I don't know how you say thank you or who you start saying thank you to, other than to everybody."

Above all, Robin loves giving credit to God for the many ways He has worked in and through Camp Barnabas.

The First Yes

When Robin looks back on the beginning of his own involvement with Camp Barnabas, it feels almost accidental. In 1994, he was working for Merrill Lynch in Springfield, Missouri. He and his wife had just moved to Monett, Missouri, and one of his friends from church was the director of Camp Soaring Hawk. Robin's friend told him about Paul and Cyndy Teas's desire to turn Camp Soaring Hawk into a camp for kids with chronic illnesses and disabilities and asked if Robin would be interested in helping them organize their efforts and start a 501(c)(3).

"I said, 'Sure, be happy to.' . . . When God said, 'Can you help?' I said, 'Yes.' That's the way we should be." He laughed. "But yeah, I had no clue, [I] just assumed that with my background in investments and finance and my education that I could be of some help. . . . It seemed like a very good idea to have a camp for children who didn't have a camp, so I was drawn by that. But to say that I knew what I was saying yes to would be a lie. I did not."

Robin distinctly remembers the moment he realized that Camp Barnabas was something special.

"I came out to Camp one night, and Cyndy Teas met me. We were walking through the old cabins, past the petting zoo that was there at the time. There used to be a big building at the end called The Lodge."

Christmas lights were strung across The Lodge's ceiling, turning the open space below into a dance floor for the Campers. Cyndy pointed to two Campers dancing together and told Robin their story. A year prior, the girl had been told that she had cancer and she wasn't likely to live another year.

And yet, there she was.

The boy she was dancing with had recently received the news that he also had cancer and might not live another year.

"Nobody on the planet knows how he feels like she does," Cyndy said to Robin.

The story shook Robin.

"[That was] the very first time that I really realized we were walking on holy ground," he said. "I thought to myself, 'This is pretty serious stuff we're dealing with. This is medicine without being medicine. It's friendship. It's touch. It's relationships. . . . We're bringing people together that have the same struggles. . . .' I think for me that was a pretty pivotal time, and I thought, 'This is really important what we're doing. It's not just a summer camp.'"

A History of Faith

Camp Barnabas has had a huge impact on the way Robin views finances and God's ability to provide.

"We've had difficulties, because you need a lot of capital to grow, especially with a property of this size. But it seems like every time we've had a need, every time we've stepped out in faith, the need was met."

This bench at Inspiration Point at Camp Barnabas was a gift from Robin's staff

Sometimes walking by faith meant getting creative to find solutions to problems. One example of this came during the early years when Camp was at capacity and the board didn't have the money to fund new cabins. Cyndy Teas told Robin about a camp she'd been to in Texas where campers stayed in yurts, and then she did a little research on whether any similar yurts were available on the market. After she found a good deal, Robin called in favors from a couple friends to help purchase two yurts for Camp.

Cyndy later told Robin that the week after the yurts were purchased was one of the best weeks of her life, because she was able to call twenty waitlisted Campers for each session and tell them Camp had space for them that summer.

"I think back on that often as I think it [was] God's provision," Robin said. "Why in the world [Cyndy] ever visited a camp in Texas with yurts, I have no idea. But it gave us the opportunity to push forward and have a little victory."

Another time, the board voted to move ahead with building a new pool, even though the project wasn't fully funded yet. One member called a contact in Washington, who agreed to donate several waterslides. Then Robin called his son, Chase, and asked if the company that Chase worked for, which installed playground equipment, might be able to help. The company agreed and donated their time for the installation.

"We had no clue that there were even slides available in Washington, had no clue how to put them in when we got them. But it's just like a lot of other businesses—you just put your head down and keep asking questions and look for the opportunity," Robin said. "That's one example of the board saying, 'Yes, we're moving forward. We don't think that we're doing anything here that God can't fix.'"

Over time, those experiences gave Robin and other board members the courage to keep stepping out in faith, trusting that God would work.

"We've [stepped out in faith] at Camp twenty times, and every single time that need has been met. For years, [we called this] 'the Barnabas spirit,' but I've reached the point where I just believe it's God's Spirit. It's just healthy and alive here."

As a board, Robin said that they've learned to seek God's will on every project they approve.

"What is it God wants us to do? That became the driving factor more than the financial picture. If God calls us to do that, we felt He was going to deliver what we needed to make that happen."

Robin recalled one board meeting when the question of finances came up in relation to a new project they were discussing.

"Yeah, but where does faith come in?" asked a newer board member.

Robin had been sitting on the edge of his seat, wanting to jump in and ask the same question, but had held back because he wanted to give newer board members a chance to speak.

"Thank you," he told that board member. "Thank you so much, because that's the history of our organization. If you're telling me that we need to make a decision today on a project that we have 60 percent of the funding, my answer is yes. Because I have faith God will deliver. If He doesn't, we'll be OK. It's not going to put us under. But isn't it nice every once in a while to say yes to God? I just feel like that pleases Him that we, in our own human way, try to be as faithful as we can."

Robin (left) with check for Camp Barnabas

Starting Something New

Camp Barnabas has also affected Robin's personal faith journey. When Camp first began, he and his family regularly attended praise and worship services with the Campers.

"We would watch the children in church, and it was like something I'd never seen. There was no pomp and circumstance to it, there was no ritual to it. It was just true worship."

Around that time, Robin also began attending events through the men's ministry Promise Keepers. Between worshiping with Camp Barnabas kids and worshiping with 75,000 other men in the Kansas City Chiefs Arrowhead Stadium, Robin said he was spoiled for ordinary church worship.

"I would go to a traditional church, and it wasn't enough."

He began to feel strongly led to plant a new church in Monett that focused on a different, more vibrant form of worship. When he decided to tell the other deacons at his current church about his decision, he didn't know what their response would be.

The oldest deacon in the group asked, "Robin, do you feel God telling you to do this, to start a new church?"

"Without question," Robin responded.

"Well, you have no choice then," the man said. "You have no choice. Do it. Go. Be successful."

Robin helped to plant Monett Community Church in 2003. Fittingly, the church that was inspired by Camp Barnabas now has a lead pastor—Todd Korasick—whose children had attended Camp and who took the job, in part, because of its proximity to Barnabas.[1]

After Thirty Years

The way of life—of trust in God and taking steps of faith—that is now familiar for Robin is very foreign to most.

"You know, a lot of us talk the talk about faith. But a lot of us keep ourselves in a position where we really don't have to exercise faith," Robin said.

After almost thirty years of involvement with Barnabas, Robin has learned to trust.

"If anything, Camp helped me develop an attitude that, given my solution to the problem or God's solution to the problem, I'd rather have God's. I believe that. And it's hard," Robin said. "But I think one thing we mostly do as individuals is we don't wait on God. The waiting is not for God, but it's for us, I think. God doesn't need us to wait on Him, but sometimes we just need to wait on God, because we mature a little bit and we learn more about waiting. I think that has helped me a lot."

---

[1] Pastor Todd Korasick's story can be read as told by his wife, Becky Korasick, in Chapter 17.

At this point, Robin is committed to the Barnabas mission for life, whether or not he continues to be on the board.

"I've said many times, 'I'll give up my seat on the board anytime.' I'm on the team already—I'm on the Barnabas team. I'm going to come visit whether I'm on the board or not."

When Robin got involved, he didn't have many friends who had children with disabilities. Now, he has dozens.

"As we've been around more and more families . . . who have special needs children, I think they have a really difficult road in life. To give them a little bit of joy, to be a part of something that gives those children a little bit of joy, is a good thing. I have pictures of myself with different Campers, and they become good friends. You know, you want the best for your friends. Anything you could do for your friends, you will do."

That is how he views Camp Barnabas's mission now—trying to help their friends.

"I won't say that [my involvement] started out as this massive mission. It really didn't. But what I realized again was the impact that it could have and the impact that it has had. Yeah, I wanna be a part of that. It goes back to what I said before—I felt like God was at work here. And if I wanted to be close to God at work, this was a good place to do it."

"Camp has allowed me to experience love and joy like no other, which is what makes this place so magical … and it is through the Campers that my faith has grown stronger. Most people would think that I'm the one helping the Campers, but in reality they are the ones helping me."

– Zoe P., Missionary

CHAPTER 7

The Best Place on Earth:
Jenn (Reier) Rodemeyer, Staff

Camp Barnabas has been Jenn (Reier) Rodemeyer's favorite place on earth since 1996.

"I will always say that's the best place on this earth—even over Disney World." Jenn laughed. "I've traveled a lot, and I still choose Camp."

A couple experiences in her early life touched her heart and prepared her for Camp Barnabas. First, in third grade, she became friends with a boy with disabilities, who ended up passing away the same year. She said that experience taught her to look at people's hearts before their outward appearances. Second, she spent several summers working at her church's summer camp as a counselor and loved every second of it.

By the time she started college, she knew she wanted to work with kids in some way. She decided to pursue a pre-med degree but wasn't sure what she would do with it.

Then, during her sophomore year, the topic of summer camps came up in a conversation with a friend from her dorm. Jenn told her friend about Faith Haven Bible Camp that she'd grown up attending in Minnesota, and her friend told her about her summers at Camp Soaring Hawk in Missouri.

"She just told me all that they did. I said, 'Oh, I would love to learn more about it,' because I'm kind of an adventurous person and willing to try something new. Her response was, 'Oh, they just recently turned it over to this Christian camp for kids with special needs . . . bummer.' And I thought, 'Bummer?! Sign me up!'"

Jenn found the phone number for Camp Barnabas and gave them a call. Cyndy Teas picked up. The memory of that call is still crystal clear, from the contrast between Jenn's Minnesotan accent and Cyndy's southern drawl, to the praise and worship music that played quietly in the background on Cyndy's end.

"We just had the most incredible conversation about their vision and their excitement for what was to come for Camp."

By the end of their conversation, Jenn knew she was interested in being part of Camp. Cyndy offered her a position as a pool director, and Jenn accepted,

Jenn and Sharon at Camp

though she would later end up switching positions when the program director resigned a week into Camp.

When Jenn told her family about her plans, their reactions were mixed. Her mom was excited for her, but her dad was concerned about whether Jenn was ready to handle the emotional heaviness that might come from working at a camp for people with chronic illnesses and disabilities. But Jenn was confident in her choice and in her ability to persevere through any difficulties that might come her way.

Jenn arrived at Camp Barnabas in 1996, the organization's first full summer at its own location.

She woke the first morning to the sound of cows mooing—a stark contrast to the city sounds she was used to. Stifling heat already filled the cabin.

"God, what am I doing here?" she prayed. But almost immediately her prayer shifted to, "God, what do you want to do with me here? Stretch me. Grow me. I'm so excited to serve."

Between that prayer and the next three summers serving at Camp Barnabas, Jenn's life would never be the same.

Close Bonds

That first summer at Camp was one of constant preparation and service. Paved pathways through Camp were still far in the future, so the team shoveled dirt and rock to make routes for the wheelchairs. She remembers sleeping rarely—only four or five hours a night. But all that work bonded them closely together.

"Still to this day, one of my closest friends . . . outside of my family is from that team that I was able to be with that first summer at Camp," Jenn said.

The environment at Camp Barnabas was unlike any Jenn had ever experienced.

"You'd walk by the pool, and there'd be three prosthetic legs sitting on the side of the pool. What other environment would that happen in? But nobody ever thought anything of it either. Nobody looked differently at anybody because they might not have a leg or arms. It was one of the most encouraging places to be."

One special friendship she developed was with a Camper named Nehemiah, whom Jenn and her family had known for many years. He had retinoblastoma, a childhood cancer that affects the eyes. In Nehemiah's case, the cancer cost him both eyes by the time he was eighteen months old. Jenn's mom taught elementary school and had Nehemiah in her class when he was in first grade, and their families had stayed in touch for several years afterward. Jenn asked if Nehemiah would want to come to Camp too. He was interested, and so for all three years that Jenn worked at Camp Barnabas, Nehemiah came as a Camper for a week each summer.

"He will always hold a special place in my heart," Jenn said. "He brought a recorder with him to Camp one year, and so his way of being part of praise and worship was playing through his recorder. . . . We spent so many fun moments together. This is a kid who wasn't afraid to do anything . . . specifically on the high ropes course. They had a tall swing at the time . . . I can't imagine going out there and doing that blind. He did it."

Jenn's family continued to stay in touch with Nehemiah's in the decades to come. When he grew up, he took a job in Denver and moved there on his own.

Jenn and Nehemiah

Nehemiah on the swing at Camp Barnabas

Eventually, he developed a brain tumor—something that unfortunately is common for people with retinoblastoma.

"My husband and I and our four kids drove out to Denver to go visit him one last time before he passed away," Jenn said. "I'm just so thankful that these kids [like Nehemiah] had the opportunity to experience Camp in some way, shape, or form before they left us here on this earth."

A Life-Changing Friendship

By the time Jenn finished her third year at Camp Barnabas, her older and younger sisters had gotten involved with Camp as well. Her older sister, Sharon, came for a week during Jenn's second year at Camp, and Jenn remembers praying beforehand that God would find a way for Sharon to be blessed by a Camper.

That Camper ended up being someone who would impact Jenn's entire family.

Hannah, age seventeen, was seriously ill with Ewing sarcoma, a rare bone cancer. But she dreamed of attending Camp. When Hannah arrived at Camp Barnabas, she and Sharon bonded quickly. Unfortunately, Hannah came down with the flu, which wreaked havoc on her already frail body. She and Sharon ended up spending most of their time in the Well House, but with the staff's help, Hannah was able to finish out her week at Camp.

After Camp, Hannah was admitted to Arkansas Children's Hospital. On one of her days off, Jenn and some other Camp staff made the four-hour drive to see her. Little did Jenn know how that visit would influence her life. During Jenn's visit, a child life specialist—a health care professional who helps kids cope with illness and injury—came to see Hannah.

"'Oh my goodness, who is this person? I need to find out,'" Jenn recalled thinking. "Hannah shared with me a little bit more about what child life [specialists do], and from that moment on, I thought, 'This is what I want to do for a career.'"

Not long after Camp ended, Hannah's doctors gave her weeks to live. Wanting to make one last trip, Hannah reached out to the Reier family to see if she could visit them in Minneapolis and go see the Mall of America.

"Little did I know Camp would come to our house." Jenn smiled.

Hannah's family drove all the way to Minneapolis from Arkansas. By the time they reached the Reier home, Hannah was struggling. She spent the night with Jenn's family and then went to the hospital for a blood transfusion the next morning. Afterward, she felt better, and Jenn, Sharon, and their younger sister, Laura, took Hannah to the Mall of America.

"We shopped till we dropped, we ate lunch, we had a blast."

But on the way home, Hannah began complaining about how her body was aching. Shortly after they reached home, Hannah fell unconscious. They called an ambulance and raced her to the hospital. Later that night, Hannah passed away.

Hannah's parents told Jenn's family afterward that they were glad she had passed away doing something she loved. A few days later, Sharon and Jenn boarded a plane to fly to Arkansas for Hannah's funeral. At the service, they sang Michael W. Smith's song "Friends"—a song they had sung many times before with Hannah, including once for a talent show at Camp Barnabas.

"I never expected my family to be involved at that level," Jenn said. "But it really taught [us] a lot about compassion. . . . I am so thankful for the opportunity Camp [provided], because [without it] we would have never grown a relationship with this family and then never got to serve in this capacity."

Serving Together

After graduating from college, Jenn married Abe Rodemeyer and moved to California to finish her graduate program as a child life specialist. She worked there for a year and a half before moving back to Minnesota to work at Mayo Clinic. Today, she is the manager of Mayo Clinic's Child Life Program.

Jenn and Abe have four children together. Though they only visited Camp Barnabas once when her oldest kids, Luke and Ella, were three and two, respectively, Camp was a common conversation topic in their family. It was enough to stir Luke's interest. When he was seventeen, Luke applied for Camp Barnabas's Apostles Program, a three-week program that includes leadership training in addition to service as a Missionary.

Luke was accepted and planned to attend in 2021, but shortly before Camp started, a Staff Member called and asked whether Luke would stay for half the summer instead of only three weeks. Luke agreed.

"I dropped him off, and immediately I thought, 'Oh, no, now I've lost him for the whole summer, and I don't know if I'm prepared for that,'" Jenn said. "But he loved it—oh my goodness, he just enjoyed it so much. I couldn't say no when he [called and said], 'Mom, I want to stay for the summer.' So he ended up staying all summer."

Luke went back to Camp in 2022 and 2023. In 2023, Ella was accepted to the Apostles Program as well. During each of the years their kids served, Jenn and Abe have also volunteered for a week in the Well House.

Even Jenn's dad got involved, having come a long way from the man who initially questioned Jenn about her emotional readiness to handle Camp.

"I encouraged him for many years—I told him, 'You've *got* to get down there.' So my dad went as a Cabin Dad. I was so proud of him. He loved it so much."

Her dad returned to Camp in fall 2022 for Barnabreak, a shortened version of Camp that occurs for one weekend each fall and spring.

"And now he shared with me he was thinking about coming for the entire summer," Jenn said. "So my dad's seventy-six years old, and he's going to come for the entire summer [in 2023]. They bought a new army truck to do paintball with the kids in the woods, and my dad's a retired cop and just has a heart to

The Rodemeyer Family at Camp in 2023

serve. He's going to go and drive the truck for the new Yeti Adventure for the entire summer.

"I said, 'See, Dad? I told you. Once you start there, you can't stop. It's an addiction.'" Jenn laughed.

A Place of Encouragement

Twenty-seven years after her first summer at Camp Barnabas, Jenn maintained that there's nowhere else quite like Barnabas, especially in terms of the encouraging environment.

She remembered frequently talking about Hebrews 3:13 with her fellow Staffers in those early summers at Camp. "But encourage one another daily, as long as it is called 'Today,' so that none of you may be hardened by sin's deceitfulness."

"That was the foundation of what I did for the first three years that I was at Camp. People lived it—they didn't just talk the talk," she said. "We'd call it the 'Barnabas Bubble,' because there's no other place like it, where you walk in and you're just surrounded by these believers who are all about being an encouragement."

Whenever she has the chance, she continues to encourage friends, family, and coworkers to go check out Camp Barnabas.

"Hey, you have a week off?" she'll ask. "Do you want to go to the coolest place on this earth?"

She smiled. "Everyone needs to go to Camp Barnabas one time in their life."

"[Camp Barnabas is] a thin place, a place where the gap between heaven and earth feels smaller. And there's no place that teaches teenagers servant discipleship better. Teenagers are stretched and challenged, and when they run dry, they learn where God picks up."

– Martin L., Cabin Parent

CHAPTER 8

Enduring Reach:
Bob Speizer, Youth Pastor

When Bob Speizer and his wife, Nancy, first took nine college students to volunteer at Camp Barnabas in 1997, he wasn't sure what to expect. A promotional video had intrigued Bob enough to get in contact with Camp Barnabas and bring a group for a week.

One of his strongest memories from that first summer was how humid it was, especially with no air conditioning in the cabins. However, when the group returned to Creekside Christian Church (then First Baptist Church of Elk Grove) in Elk Grove, California, the full impact of Camp Barnabas quickly became apparent. The church arranged an evening service to allow the students to share their experiences with the rest of the congregation.

"Everyone who shared ended up crying, because their experience was so profound," Bob said. "I thought, 'Well, we have something here.'"

Bob, who was Creekside's youth pastor at the time, continued to take students to Camp Barnabas every summer for the next nineteen years. Bob's most recent summer at Camp was in 2016, but Creekside continues to send groups today in 2023. Bob estimates that at least 1,000 high school and college students from his church have volunteered at Camp.

Bob knows of students who met their spouses at Camp and others who went into special education, disability ministries, or pastoral ministries after volunteering there. A few students even wrote books that included inspiration from their time at Camp Barnabas. One year, four of Bob's former students who had gone on to become pastors all brought groups to Camp alongside Bob and his youth group. Bob marveled at that legacy.

"It was like, 'Wow.' And they were from different states," he said. "I've heard so many people say, 'Once you're in the Barnabas family, you're in. You don't leave.'"

Widespread Impact

Camp Barnabas has had a huge impact on Bob's twenty-six years as a youth pastor.

"Along with a few of our overseas trips . . . [our trips to Camp were] the best things we did in our youth ministry," Bob said. "And I think Camp Barnabas, as far as our church [as a whole] was the best thing we did."

Camp Barnabas impacted not just the youth, but also their families, the chaperons, and those who financially supported the teams. When the church held an event to watch the *Extreme Makeover: Home Edition* episode about Camp, five hundred people showed up.

"They'd never been to Barnabas, but they lived Barnabas through our experiences. So it really ignited our whole church," Bob said. "Went way beyond anything I anticipated that first time I saw that video . . . had no way of knowing, had no way of knowing."

Among the students who came to Camp, some experienced big life changes, such as a calling to work in ministry or special ed. Others experienced smaller changes of the heart that were no less significant, even if they were less outwardly visible.

"I can't tell you how many girls would say to me . . . 'You know, I worry about my makeup or how I look or if I've got a zit . . . [but] I go [to Camp Barnabas] and I'm around these kids and teenagers who have multiple disabilities who have such joy,'" Bob remembered. "So one of the lessons that universally was learned is that, first of all, God doesn't make mistakes. Secondly, 'My problems? They're nonsense. They're absolute nonsense. I don't need to worry about that. I spent way too much time worrying about my own looks or those types of things. And I need to . . . be a lot more concerned about the inside than the outside.'"

Camp has a unique way of teaching the importance of looking at the heart instead of outward appearances.

"I've seen the most beautiful people in the world at Camp Barnabas, who, much of society, if they saw them walking down the street . . . out of discomfort or ignorance, they would cross the road," Bob said. "I can't teach the lessons about self-image, or [how] God says . . . we're all wonderfully and beautifully made, and God doesn't make mistakes. [I] could talk about that. But [students] go to Camp Barnabas, and then [they] live it."

One student's story of heart change still lingers in Bob's memory.

"[Ryan] was a football player, and he was all-conference tight end for our Thundering Herd, [the] Elk Grove High School football team. He was also on the basketball team, later went on to a college basketball scholarship, scored sixty-seven points in one game. Anyway, he was quite an athlete. . . . There's nothing he couldn't do."

But at the end of Ryan's first day at Camp, he approached Bob. "I don't think I can do this," he said.

"I don't think you can either," Bob responded. "But I know God can use you. God can do it through you and strengthen you for the task."

Ryan submitted to Bob's advice, and by the end of the week, he had developed a close relationship with his Camper.

Camp Barnabas in 1998

"I'd never seen him cry before, but he cried when he left his student at the end of the week," Bob said. "God did some amazing things in his life. . . . He would say today this was one of the most important things that's happened in his life."

Ryan's story stands out to Bob because of the magnitude of the change, but similar things happened to many of his students.

"There are many who said, 'I can't do this,' in the first or second day, or, 'I didn't sign up for this—I got a student who doesn't like me and who [tells me] that,'" Bob remembered. "So the process of the faith-walk as the week goes on and loving on that kid unconditionally . . . they had to learn the power of prayer, that it wasn't their strength, but God's strength, [and] also just persevering."

Lessons Taught by Experience

As a youth pastor, the best thing for Bob about taking his students to Camp Barnabas were the many lessons they learned that he could never teach from a pulpit.

"I can't teach those lessons to our kids about losing themselves by serving someone else, getting out of their comfort zone."

As news about the trips to Camp Barnabas spread through their church, Bob did his best to make sure students understood the more difficult aspects of the trip and not just the fun experiences shown in promotional videos.

"We wanted our students to be prepared," Bob said. "I would start out going, 'Well, they've got a lot of mosquitoes, they've got chiggers, it's really humid, you sweat a lot. It's going to be the hardest, best week of your life.'"

But he also encouraged them, when they came face-to-face with those difficulties, to give them to God.

"It's just profound how they have to work through things. I think that helps them in life. They have to work through disappointment, have to work through things, at least initially, not being what they thought they would be," he said. "We would tell them, 'Don't come with a lot of expectations. God will meet you there. But just kind of leave your expectations. Give them to God, and He'll meet you there.'"

Bob witnessed exponential growth in the faith of students who took that message to heart.

"They've never prayed so much in their life. They get there, they're praying all the time because they're having a difficult time," he said. "In the essence of doing that, they learn a lot more about themselves and about just trusting God for His strength. And if they can do it there, that enables them to come back home and to continue that. Almost every student I've had has strengthened their walk by going to Camp Barnabas."

Perhaps most importantly, Bob saw students learn how to give and receive unconditional love.

"The world blares at them that [they] need to look this way, act this way. Then they go to this week at Camp Barnabas, and everything is thrown away," he said. "They see life as it should be, that we treat people not based on how they look or even how they act—just as Christ does us. We're pretty unsavory people a lot of the time, but He loves us. He forgives us, gives us grace and mercies that are new every day. . . . God loves us unconditionally. . . . He lavishes everything on us. That lesson is amazing."

Putting Life in Perspective

Bob has witnessed Camp Barnabas's profound effect on his own life and the lives of his family members as well.

"I think the same lessons that kids learned, I learned. I just turned seventy. As I age, I have to deal with my own frailties," he said. "But it puts life in perspective—that God has gifted us; He's made us how He's made us. I think it helps me to live every day with a purpose. To look at my trials, I put them in perspective, because I know some people have gone through a lot more trials than I have. I really learned that at Camp Barnabas."

He got to see this firsthand the year that he asked Cyndy Teas to pair him with a student as a one-on-one buddy.

"I was always a Cabin Dad except the third year [when] I said, 'I want to have a student. . . . Then I can tell my students that I did it too.'"

Bob was paired with a Camper named Elijah. Because his needs were complex, a second aide, a college student from Texas Tech, was assigned to Elijah as well.

"We would have to bathe him. We'd have to feed him."

Sadly, Elijah has passed away since their time together at Camp, but Bob will always remember the experience of getting to serve Elijah.

"Man, that taught me a lot," he said.

Students from Bob's church praying together at Camp

Bob's wife and all his kids got to experience Camp too.

"My wife's a nurse, and she's been there multiple times on the nursing Staff," Bob said. "Our son and his wife and our daughter and her husband have been on Staff there. . . . Our daughter didn't meet her husband there, but their relationship bloomed there, because they worked on Staff there, they saw each other there. They saw characteristics that they liked in each other."

Though Bob hasn't been to Camp Barnabas in a few years, he hopes to go back someday and take his entire family.

"My dream is . . . to take my granddaughters when they hit high school age or when they're thirteen or fourteen and have my son and daughter and their spouses [there too]. My son-in-law is a doctor, so he'll be a doctor on Staff. My wife, who knows, [maybe] she'll still [volunteer as] a nurse. . . . I don't know what I will be, but our son and our daughter [and daughter-in-law] will be a Cabin Dad and Mom[s]. And then our granddaughters will all be in cabins as Counselors, so all eleven of us—I've got five granddaughters—all eleven of us will get to go to Camp Barnabas together."

His granddaughters are still young, so the dream is several years from fruition, but it's one Bob holds onto.

"I will be very old by that time . . . [but] I could do it. That would be amazing."

"It's really fun to connect with [student nurses] and to teach them . . . and to see them come back and be full-fledged nurses and to make it through the week without the instructor and grow in confidence. Because sometimes they'll come back the next summer right when they're a brand-new nurse. They'll just grow in confidence in their nursing skills and put into practice things that they learned the year before."

– Mary B., Nurse

CHAPTER 9

Unexpected Gifts:
Glenda Blevins, Nurse

A million little things represent Camp Barnabas in Glenda Blevin's memory: open mics at mealtimes, the soothing sound of Cyndy Teas's voice, stiffened hair from shampoo that won't wash out due to hard water, the humor that kept the Well House doctors and nurses sane through crazy days, and the uninhibited way Campers and volunteers would dance at Wrap Up every night.

Glenda first met Paul and Cyndy Teas at her church in 1999 when Paul got up to ask for prayer on a Sunday morning. Glenda had noticed Paul and Cyndy a few weeks before but had yet to meet them.

"There was this movie star-looking, white-haired man and his adorable wife, and I thought, 'Where did these people come from?'" Glenda said. "You know, I live in a small, sort of redneck community, and I thought, 'These people ooze class.' Yet they were humble and didn't say much."

That Sunday, Paul explained his and Cyndy's work at Camp Barnabas and said that many of their donations had recently dried up. He asked the congregation to pray for God's provision.

Glenda had heard of Camp Barnabas and went to talk to Paul afterward about volunteering as a nurse. Her first summer serving at Camp was in 2000.

"Talk about magical," Glenda said. "It was very rough back then. We didn't have the fancy gate, and we just had [a dirt road] drive in. The only air-conditioned building was the one the nurses stayed in. And yet, it was just—I swear it just captured your heart."

Glenda was experiencing great upheaval in her own life at the time. She had just gone through a divorce and, in her own words, "wasn't feeling too good about myself." To come to Camp and see all the Campers who were comfortable in their own bodies, regardless of their disabilities, was a gift Glenda didn't know she needed.

"Everybody says, 'Aren't you nice to go help all those poor disabled people?' Nope, they are there to heal the sick people who come to volunteer. We don't even know we're sick all the time," she explained. "After that week . . . come spring the next year, it is like a call to Mecca. I mean, you're just hungering for that whole experience again."

Camp gates, 2000

Lifelong Friendships

Like many other volunteers from the early days, Glenda found that the rough conditions at Camp—no air-conditioning, no hot water for showers, no windows to shut when storms rolled through—worked to bond the Staff and volunteers together.

Many of the friends Glenda made at Camp continue to be friends today. One of those friends is Ellen Beary, a retired school nurse from St. Louis who still comes to volunteer each summer and brings her daughter, Allison, who started out as a Camper but now volunteers in the Well House.

"[Allison] does not live independently, but she is what I call a spiritual savant," Glenda said. "She [goes] up to people with a word, and I [always say], 'When Allison speaks, you need to listen, because she's anointed with a word for you.'"

Today, whenever Glenda goes to St. Louis, she'll visit Allison and Ellen, and when Allison and Ellen come to Camp Barnabas for two-week stints as volunteers, they stay with Glenda on the weekend between sessions.

"We have just really attached. Do we agree on every little thing in our lives? . . . No, but we are united in . . . [the fact that] we both want good [in the world]."

Many other relationships made through Camp have affected Glenda's life as well. One Camper named Minda, who was born without legs and had only partial arms, won Glenda's heart.

"She was beautiful, just beautiful. I used to say, 'Minda, I get lost in your eyes,'" Glenda remembered. "She graduated from Southwest Baptist University with an art degree. . . . I have one of [her paintings in] my bedroom. Absolutely charming. She painted by holding [the brush] between her neck and her shoulder. . . . She danced—oh, dances at Barnabas. . . . [Campers] would boogie the night away. Minda danced by wiggling her whole [torso] in her wheelchair. And I mean, she'd go crazy with the music. . . . She impacted us so much."

Cassie, a young woman with autism from Glenda's church, helped illustrate to Glenda the gift that Camp Barnabas gave to families. Cassie, who was in her late twenties when she first came to Camp, had never spent a night away from her parents. Glenda remembers Cassie's parents were fully expecting to need to come pick up Cassie from Camp, assuming that the new environment would be too much for her to handle.

"Well, needless to say, we did not call her parents. . . . At the time, they had stables with horses. Her mother said, 'Keep her away from the horses. She's terrified of them,'" Glenda remembered. "When they came to pick her up, guess what her favorite thing was? She couldn't stop talking about the horses."

Today, Cassie's parents frequently remind Glenda not to mention Camp Barnabas around Cassie, because the instant anyone brings it up—even if Camp is still months away—Cassie won't be able to stop asking questions about it.

Glenda (center) with two of her fellow nurses at Camp

"[Cassie would say] 'We're going to Camp Barnabas? When is Cassie going to Camp Barnabas?' You know, just over and over—it drives her parents nuts." Glenda smiled. "They have that week now to spend with their family, with their [other] children. . . . It's wonderful to give people that week."

Glenda remains incredibly grateful for her many years of friendship with Paul and Cyndy Teas as well.

"[Paul and Cyndy] would adopt people into their lives," Glenda said. "They adopted so many people into their lives, and it was like, who am I? You know, what do I bring to the table? But they adopted me. I was there for their daughter's wedding—magical, magical wedding."

She remembers how frequently Paul and Cyndy took Camp families or volunteers into their home, however inconvenient it might be.

"They were so giving. That was such a lesson, an example to all of us," she said. "When they came for a visit last summer and went to Camp, they stayed with me. What a privilege. What a privilege."

Deep Convictions

Through Camp Barnabas, Glenda has learned to appreciate each gift that various people bring to the table. For example, she remembers being extremely humbled by the sacrifice of the many construction workers who took time off work to be part of the remodeling projects at Camp Barnabas during the filming of the episode for *Extreme Makeover: Home Edition*. She remembers seeing many construction workers tear up through interactions with the Campers or Staff, but the thought that made her cry was that these workers were giving up their "milk money."

"I worked for the federal government as a nurse and I was there on vacation time, so I was getting paid while I was there," she said. "[These people] were not being paid to be there, and that, to me, is the greatest gift. . . . The only reward [for them] was in their hearts. They're the heroes. I think that's one thing you learn at Barnabas . . . is the heroes among us aren't the people that you see on TV representing the Camp. It's those people that God knows about, nobody else knows, [and] you learn to appreciate everybody else's gift."

Glenda also gained a deep conviction about the beauty and value of every individual.

"[People with disabilities] are a gift . . . [and] if you don't open the gift, you miss what's inside," she said. "It is like . . . finding a flower in the field. You gotta go. You gotta go interact. It is just, there's something really special there."

Camp Barnabas helped shape Glenda's faith as well. Prayer has become something that is not only deeply meaningful for her but necessary to deal with the challenges of life.

"When catastrophe comes or fear comes . . . prayer is your first line of defense, versus maybe getting mad about it, or [saying], 'Woe is me.' You go to prayer. Prayer is your first line of defense in facing something more than you feel you can handle.

Cabins at Camp Barnabas in the early 2000s

"We did a lot of group prayer. . . . Some people come [to Camp] with faiths that are very conservative, very personal. You don't talk about it. You're not demonstrative. [Then] you let down some of those old strongholds, those guards that keep you from experiencing the fullness of faith. That's what Barnabas teaches, that I think if I had to nutshell it—it shows you the fullness of faith. Can you find it other places? I'm sure. But at Barnabas, it's a guarantee."

Ordained Connections

After twenty-three years of volunteering with Camp, Glenda has seen its influence not just on her own heart but also on her family. She saw it soften her son's heart toward people with disabilities. She saw it become a safe haven for her grandson, first as a Camper when he was diagnosed with leukemia and then later when he became a volunteer.

"It's more than just entertainment or a project—it's ordained."

Perhaps the biggest change she saw was in the life of one of her granddaughters. At the time, her granddaughter was fifteen and had developed a generally negative attitude toward life. When she came to visit Glenda, it happened to be during a time period when Paul and Cyndy Teas were coming back to visit Camp. Glenda wanted to go see them, so she told her granddaughter that she needed to come along. She didn't have to talk to anyone—she could bring a book and sit in the Well House, Glenda assured her—but she needed to come.

However, after getting a tour of Camp and hanging out with the nurses in the Well House for a little while, her granddaughter was struck by everyone's friendliness. When Glenda came back after visiting Paul and Cyndy, her granddaughter met her with the words: "I already called Mom—I told her to sign me up as a volunteer."

When her week to volunteer arrived, Glenda's granddaughter started having second thoughts. She asked Glenda to call her dad and see if he'd let her come home. He didn't, and one of the Staff Members assured Glenda, "Once she connects with a Camper who needs her, she's going to be OK."

By Wednesday, that connection happened, and Glenda's granddaughter became an example to many of the transformation Camp Barnabas has a way of instigating.

"I mean, she was known around Camp as this long-faced [girl] . . . who suddenly blossomed. She left Camp and went to a nursing home and offered to volunteer. . . . She's now at the University of Missouri, and she called me last night. . . . She said, 'Grandma, I really want to go into nursing.'" Glenda smiled. "See that evolution? It wasn't something I looked for, but last night, it was like we've come full circle here."

For Glenda personally, Camp Barnabas continues to be a place of connection and community. At seventy-seven, she no longer works as a nurse, but she volunteers at the Well House for a few days each summer.

"My job is my OCD unleashed. I go get up—and old people wake up early, by the way. They don't sleep in. So, by six, I usually had all the floors mopped with a type of bleach water. It smells so clean, and I would pick up all the trash. That's what I do, that and laundry. I love laundry. . . . And I redid all these linen closets, because those are critical to operation. Oh, they were works of art."

Glenda is grateful that Camp Barnabas allows her to continue finding ways to serve.

"They find jobs for us, so that we can just gracefully age out at Camp. I appreciate that. You love just being part of a team," she said. "There's something for [everyone with] willing hands."

"You are not alone. At Camp Barnabas, people won't judge you for the way you are.... Once I started going, I felt closer to Jesus than when I stayed at home.... If you feel lost and alone, go to Camp Barnabas. There's nothing but care out there."

– Justin T., Camper

CHAPTER 10

Continued Transformation:
Daniel Townsend, Summer Staff

When Daniel Townsend reminisces about his first summer working at Camp Barnabas in 2002 at age nineteen, he wonders if he might have been the least qualified person Barnabas ever hired.

"I was one of only about two or three of the seventy Staffers that summer who didn't have previous experience with special needs kids," he said. "[For] everybody else, this was just all old hat . . . which is good on the one hand, because I had a lot of people I could go to for advice. On the other hand, I felt super intimidated. . . . Apparently, I looked pretty nervous, because later that summer, Cyndy [Teas] told me that she really didn't expect me to make it through the summer."

Daniel heard about Camp Barnabas through a friend from college who had worked there the previous summer. Daniel wasn't initially interested, but when his friend continued to encourage him to consider it, he decided to apply. By the end of the lengthy application process, his interest had grown, and he was excited to hear he had been hired.

He was able to ease into Camp with a week of Campers who were fairly independent. Daniel was paired with a young man who had Down syndrome, who—though hard to keep track of at times—was very sweet.

"It was a fun week, and it kind of just broke the ice."

The next week, Daniel met a Camper who would change his entire perspective on life. Zac was a ten-year-old who had cerebral palsy. Going into the summer, Daniel had wondered if many of the Campers would be somewhat somber—weighed down with the difficulties they faced in life. But Zac blew those expectations out of the water.

"It was his first week at Camp, so it was a new experience for him," Daniel said. "He just loved everything . . . and was super excited about everything. He made a huge impression on me, because he was extremely disabled and couldn't take care of his own needs without assistance . . . but he was just the happiest, sweetest kid. . . . I could never fathom how a kid with that many disabilities could just be so happy."

Daniel with Zac, 2003 Inspiration Point

In a speech he later wrote about his experiences at Camp, Daniel said of Zac: "If he could be that way, what business did I have in being such a grouch? The whole past year, I'd spent sulking about this and that, especially girl problems, making a martyr of myself. But I could talk, walk, see, hear, breathe, and a million other little miracles that I'd never stopped to thank God for. Zac totally blasted my view of the world and replaced it with something beautiful. I'll be grateful to him for that as long as I live."

A Unique Bond

Although Daniel didn't have experience working with kids with disabilities before volunteering at Camp Barnabas, he did have unique life experiences that made him more compassionate toward their circumstances.

When Daniel was young, he'd experienced several health issues, most of which stemmed from a condition he was born with called subglottic stenosis, which meant his airway was too narrow. A baby's airway is typically the width of their little finger, Daniel explained, but his was merely the width of pencil lead. In order to help him breathe, Daniel needed a tracheostomy tube (or trach), a tube surgically inserted into the trachea to keep the airway open. Daniel had a trach until he was about two years old and continued to have breathing problems up until he was seven or eight.

"I can't really say how often, but it was very common as a young kid to wake up at night unable to breathe and have to get an ambulance to go to the hospital and get an oxygen tent," Daniel said. "It just kind of felt normal, you know—it was just life."

Daniel also struggled with some obsessive-compulsive tendencies and a number of sensory issues, often feeling overwhelmed by loud and chaotic environments.

"I don't know if there's any connection between my breathing problems and this heightened sensitivity to my surroundings, but it would make sense if there was."

He learned as an adult that his mom had him tested for autism at age four. Though he didn't quite qualify for that or for a sensory processing disorder, the symptoms still played a large part in his daily life—enough to give him a strong sense of camaraderie and an extra dose of empathy for Campers who struggled with similar issues.

One Camper Daniel formed a deep connection with was twelve-year-old Justin Thompkins, whom Daniel met during his first year at Barnabas. Having initially signed up to work only the first half of the summer, Daniel had such a great time that he decided to come back and volunteer for a couple more weeks at the end of the summer. For one of those weeks, he was paired with Justin, a long-time Camper.

Justin is partially deaf and has glaucoma. He also has neurofibromatosis, a rare condition that, in Justin's case, causes tumors and requires him to have a trach. Daniel had never met someone who still had a trach and was eager to share his own health experiences with Justin.

"The night before he came, all the other people there who knew him kept telling me I was the luckiest person there, because I was going to be working

Justin and Daniel

with him.... So I'm waiting down there to meet him as he gets off the bus [from the Missouri School for the Blind]. And I'm about five-foot-two—I'm pretty short. So he hops off the bus, and he pats me on the head. He's like, 'Why are you so short?' That's his first word to me. I'm like, 'Nice to meet you too.'" Daniel laughed. "He gets his stuff off the bus, and he goes to the cabin. He unloads all his stuff. And he asks if we have a CD player, and I'm like, 'Yeah, we do,' because CDs were still pretty common back then. And the very first thing he does before he unpacks anything—[he] gets his Chubby Checker CD out and puts it in and does 'The Twist.' That's just what he wanted to do first thing. And then he fills up his water gun and goes to the conference room and squirts his brother. He was just all over the place. Just such a fun kid."

Because of Justin's trach, he wasn't able to submerge himself in the pool, which was disappointing for him. Daniel made it his mission that week to encourage him.

"I would try to say, 'Justin, I think it's really cool you have a trach,' and I would let him feel my trach scar. I don't know if he'd ever met anybody who had a trach like him and didn't have it anymore. So he thought it was kind of cool that he could feel that hole in my neck, and that was just kind of fun," Daniel said. "Throughout the week, I would say, 'Justin, you're really cool, because you have a trach.' And so by the end of the week, I would say, 'Justin, why are you so cool?' And he would say, 'Because I have a trach.' So that was really special. That was kind of a point of bonding for both of us."

Walking the Walk

Involvement with Camp Barnabas made a big difference in Daniel's faith. It showed him that Christianity doesn't just mean having the right ideas or beliefs—it requires getting your hands dirty serving other people.

"You learn more by serving other people than you do by reading books," Daniel said.

Camp also gave him opportunities to share his faith and learn how to communicate it.

"From the very beginning, Paul and Cyndy viewed Camp as being a place to make sure kids have fun, but the main thing, the number one thing that all of us were told was our main job, was to make sure that Campers went home knowing God loved them.... I think having that as the main focus created a lot of unity on the Staff, because we all had the same purpose."

But in the end, Daniel was just as deeply impacted by the Campers' faith as they might have been by his. Justin's faith, especially, impressed Daniel.

"I feel like I learned more from him than I'd ever learned my whole life in Sunday school. And he wasn't even trying to teach me . . . he just did by being who he was."

In the speech about his experiences at Camp, Daniel reflected on Justin's faith. "I remember sitting on the porch of the dining hall, praying for [Justin] to be able to see again and to be rid of his trach. He prayed, not casually, but as if he really believed God could heal him. Justin was teaching me so much about trusting in God. I shed most of my serious medical problems as a child. Could I be as content as Justin if they had followed me into my teenage years? I knew I couldn't. Justin was a better man than me."

Twenty Years of Change

Daniel stayed involved with Camp Barnabas for several more years until a move and full-time job made it harder. The list of ways Camp impacted him is long.

"For starters, I wouldn't be doing what I'm doing right now career-wise if not for Camp Barnabas. I don't even know what I would have ended up doing, had I not been to Camp."

Daniel with Zac, Summer 2023

Daniel was a journalism major in college and worked for a newspaper and a magazine for a little while. But after his experience at Camp Barnabas, his work felt like it was missing something.

"The only thing I could really imagine doing that would be fulfilling would be working with [people with] disabilities," he said. "By the second summer [at Camp], I just couldn't imagine being happy doing anything else."

Today, he works at The Mustard Seed, a community for adults with intellectual disabilities in Mississippi.

Daniel thinks being surrounded by enthusiastic and extroverted Staff Members helped shape his personality too.

"I'm a very shy person. I'm still shy, but it did bring me out of my shell for a bit, because I mean, most of the Staff at Camp had no capacity to be embarrassed. They were just a wild, wild group. And that was just very eye-opening."

His friendship with Justin has continued to be an important part of his life too. The summer after Daniel got married, Justin stayed with him and his wife, Michelle, over a weekend between two Camp sessions.

"He kind of jokingly called us his other parents, and he got my wife to tuck him in. He really loved getting to be our guest. He went home and was talking about how my wife was a much better cook than his dad was. That's just kind of become a thing—he calls us his other parents, and he'll call Michelle on Mother's Day. When my daughter, Joy, was born, he came down to meet her, and he kept referring to her as his little sister," Daniel said. "It's kind of just come to feel like he's a member of the family."

Today, Daniel can't imagine what his life would be like if it weren't for Camp Barnabas.

"I shudder to think what my life would be like had I not gotten involved at Camp Barnabas all those years ago," he said in his speech. "It's changed me, and I would like to think it's still changing me. Every time I go there, I feel refreshed, like God is giving me a big hug. It doesn't get much better than that."

"Living for other people brings so much joy. Serving other people every moment, showing Jesus to them, knowing them deeply . . . it gives you a new perspective. I realized things about God and myself and other people I hope to never forget."

– Vella K., Missionary

CHAPTER 11

Perspective Shifts and Life Changes:
Mike Mrosko, Camp Director

As the director of Camp Barnabas, Mike Mrosko spends the summers as a fireman and the other nine months of the year as a mender of nets.

"The year to year is very much a jetstream into summer, and then in the summertime, my role shifts to coaching, training, and reacting," Mike explained. "If [most] of the year I'm planning and building, then ideally in May I'm training. I'm doing enormous amounts of [coaching the Staff], 'OK, here's everything you need to know,' so that when Camp starts, I can just start moving to the fires. . . . In the summer, I play a fireman role, whereas the rest of the year, I'm recruiting and polishing and mending the nets so that we can do it again and do it even better than before."

Growing up in Amarillo, Texas, Mike never would have guessed that his path would lead here, to Barnabas. He wouldn't have classified himself as a church kid, though he attended occasionally. But in sixth grade, he met his best friend, Alan, who became like a brother.

"I'd go to his house and sit around the table and have a family meal together. They'd pray together, they'd laugh together—they did all this stuff I wasn't super accustomed to in my home," Mike remembered.

Mike attended a summer camp for the first time with Alan, and after high school graduation, they both moved to College Station, Texas, to attend Texas A&M, though Mike still had some prerequisites he needed to complete first before he could be accepted. Around that time, they also both applied to be camp counselors at a summer camp in Texas. Alan was accepted, and Mike was not.

"I was devastated," Mike said, shaking his head.

Knowing Mike's disappointment, Alan offered to buy him coffee at the coffee shop where he worked. When they pulled into the parking lot, Alan said, "I want to pray for you. I know God's got something for you."

The memory stands out vividly in Mike's mind.

"He said a very simple prayer of, 'God, I just pray that you would show Mike what you have for him. Just make his paths straight. In Jesus' name, amen.' I

Mike with Camper

was still bitter at my situation. I wasn't in a great headspace to really receive that prayer, and to take in the blessing my friend was giving me. I was like, 'Thanks, whatever,' and we went into the coffee shop."

While Alan went behind the counter to start making him some coffee, Mike noticed a couple guys buying very large canisters of coffee. Curious, Mike struck up a conversation.

"Man, you guys must really like this coffee," he said.

"Yeah, we do," one of them said, "but we're just stocking up for the road."

"Oh, where are you from?"

"We're from Missouri. We're doing some recruiting down here."

Even more curious now, Mike said, "You're a long way from Missouri. What are you recruiting for?"

"We're recruiting for a summer camp," one of the men said.

Mike's jaw dropped.

"We've got one more male Staff slot open. Are you interested?"

Staggered, Mike could barely get his questions out. "Yeah, absolutely! What do I—uh, I don't know if I'm interested. I don't even know your camp. What's it like?"

The man—Paul Morris, who was the director of Camp Barnabas at the time—gave Mike an interview on the spot, and by the end of the conversation, the deal was sealed. Mike took the last male Staff slot for Camp Barnabas in the summer of 2005.

The Journey to Director

That first summer at Camp Barnabas changed Mike's life.

"It blew me away," he said. "I saw messy Christians who were just trying to figure out what it looked like to follow God and be obedient and listen to Him . . . while also loving and serving others and not looking at themselves all the time. I saw that in real and radical ways, and it changed my life forever."

Mike remembers thinking that someday he would love to run a camp for people with disabilities, but he never dreamed that would become a reality.

In 2006, Mike returned to Camp as a Summer Staff Member. Then at the end of the summer, founders Paul and Cyndy Teas asked Mike to stay on as the retreat coordinator, a role in which he would work with groups that wanted to use the Camp's facilities during the off-season for anything from church retreat groups to weddings to class reunions.

Mike was thrilled to accept, thinking this new role might open up a whole career for him. However, after two years, Mike found himself burnt out. The retreat coordinator role was fulfilling, but it was also exhausting, and Mike left Staff in April 2009, unsure he would ever work in ministry again.

But in the spring of 2011, he and his bride-to-be, Crystal, came to Barnabas to visit, so that Mike could show her the place that had meant so much to him. Due to a few new programs as well as some personal crises in the lives of a couple of Staff Members, Camp was in a tough spot at the time. After their visit, Paul Teas reached out and asked if there was any chance Mike could come back to help for the summer.

With their wedding coming up at the end of the summer and lots of planning to do in the meantime, Mike left the decision up to Crystal. Crystal said it seemed like Barnabas could use Mike's help, so they both agreed he would help however he could. Camp put Mike to work in the office.

"I was the palest person at Camp. I mean, you very rarely saw me out of the office. I'd step out to talk to a Missionary or Camper and step back in to try to plan for the next week," Mike recalled. "And then I'd be on the phone with my fiancée trying to plan a wedding. Right after I left Camp—literally, it was like five days later—I got married."

By this time, Mike had a good understanding of the inner workings of Camp. That dream of starting a camp returned, and Mike began the process of launching a 501(c)(3). During that time, he talked often with Jason Brawner, Barnabas's operations director, asking why Barnabas did things like this, or had they ever thought about doing that.

In 2012, Jason called Mike and told him that Barnabas was going through some big changes. Paul and Cyndy Teas were leaving, and Jason was taking over as CEO. He wanted Mike to come back, fill the operations director role, and begin implementing some of his ideas at Camp.

"That's awesome. I'm super flattered, but let me pray about it and discuss this with my wife," Mike replied.

After praying about it, Crystal's response was simple: "When are we going?" she asked.

Mike has been working at Barnabas ever since, filling a variety of roles. In early 2020, he became the camp director, and he and Crystal moved to live at Camp year-round.

"It's like the movie *We Bought a Zoo*," Mike said. "Who lives at camp? We do."

He laughed as he recalled the unique habits his kids have picked up from living at Camp Barnabas. "In restaurants they'll try to start banging on plates, and we're like, 'Oh, no, no, please don't do that.' Or in Walmart, they'll try to talk to everybody, or they'll chant to people, and those things are super fun, but it's just this weird moment in our lives. My wife and I will remind each other all the time that we're living the good old days. Because again, who lives at camp?"

Mike's day-to-day routines are rarely the same, with the most drastic changes coming between the summer months when he's responding to Staff, Camper, and volunteer needs and the other months when he plans for the summer. He sees his role as both an honor and a responsibility, and he loves getting to play a part in the wonder of Camp.

"It's my goal that any Camper, regardless of ability or disability, would be able to come in the gates of Barnabas and say, 'Wow, I get to be *here*?' Or, 'Wow, they built that for *me*? That's where I'm staying? I get to play there? I get to fish there?' Everything we have here shouldn't just be an accessible thing or a thing for people with disabilities. It should be this thing of wonder and beauty and awe, that anybody would say, 'Wow, that is *magical*. What is *that*?' Because everyone deserves that in their life, and so many of our population, they never get to experience that."

A Change in Perspective

For Mike, being camp director gives him a front row seat to life change.

"When you get someone who has been left out and looked at as different and has all these challenges, and you pair them with somebody who has been given every opportunity in the world and somehow isn't satisfied . . . there's something beautiful that happens," he said. "It just changes both of them."

Because of a human tendency toward selfishness, Mike believes the work of Camp Barnabas would collapse without Jesus at the center.

"It would be too hard; it would be too much. But then you throw in this calling to be here—this, 'I can't do it without You, [God]' moment. Then . . . your perception starts to shift. These people you thought of as different aren't that different after all. They may have different challenges or different abilities, but they're still God's children.

"[Barnabas is] this unique thing God uses to take people who have viewed people with disabilities as a charity their whole life—or even as something scary, like [they would] avoid them in an aisle at Walmart, because they're making so much noise—then they go to Barnabas and realize, 'Whoa, I had it all wrong.'

Mike (right) with the cross from Inspiration Point

Suddenly, the Lord used Barnabas to change their whole perception to, 'Man, this person is incredible. I'm the wreck. I'm the mess. How can this person who has nothing and can't even move their legs be so happy, and I have everything and I'm miserable?' This realization tends to happen."

Mike had a perspective-shifting moment of his own in the summer of 2022.

"I was exhausted. A lot of stuff had been going a little haywire, a little wonky. I'd just been running around like crazy for the past couple days. I hadn't drunk enough water . . . and I was starting to get a migraine."

He was discussing a problem with a few other Staff Members outside the dining hall when a group of girls approached, all laughing and talking loudly.

Mike knew one of them—E.J., who is deaf. She came up to Mike and signed "bearded man," her sign name for him.

"She's like, 'Mike, Mike.' She doesn't pay attention to anyone else. Because she's deaf, that means whatever she's looking at, she's paying attention to. That's the thing in focus. Nothing around her matters. So she has completely interrupted whatever conversation I was in. I'm just smiling now, in my pain and anguish, because of just how big her entrance was."

"Can I give you something?" she asked Mike.

"Yeah, E.J., anything."

E.J. tapped her Missionary, who pulled out a bag of tiny rubber duckies.

"This is a friendship duck," E.J. told Mike. "Now we can always be friends forever."

Touched, Mike said, "This is awesome. Thank you so much, E.J."

"No problem." Then she turned and left.

That night, Mike was holding the duck while talking with one of the camp doctors.

"Oh, you got a duck!" the doctor said. "I haven't gotten one. You're part of the friendship duck club."

"I *am*," Mike said, squeaking the toy in one hand. "I somehow made it into this elite club."

"Yeah, I was pretty hesitant about E.J. coming to Camp," the doctor said.

When he saw Mike's confusion, he went on to explain that E.J. has a rare condition that can cause severe health complications at almost any moment. She was on waitlists for several organs, and unless a cure is found, E.J. is unlikely to live past forty.

Hearing more about E.J.'s condition was a turning point for Mike.

"I'm squeaking this toy she gave me because I'm in this forever friendship club, and I'm just visualizing the joy that this group of girls [has] because of E.J., and the way she came over to me—who's having all these self-centered thoughts, who's thinking only about himself and how to make things easier—and she gives me a friendship duck," he recalled.

"And I'm like, 'That's it.' We get inside our heads so much, thinking things like, 'I wish this was better,' or 'I wish we could do that differently,' or 'Why didn't God let this happen?' But why did God allow a little girl to be born [with severe health concerns] who then gets to go around so stinking happy and make people's *day*? And here I am worried about *what*? What am I really worried about?... [It's] moments like these that put life in perspective."

Mike smiled. He hopes many others can experience the joy of being in the friendship club with E.J.

"I can't make any promises. It's up to her," he said. "But I still keep that duck."

Part 2

"At other camps, it's a week about ourselves, but at Barnabas, it's a whole week of getting to let people with special needs have the best week ever. It's a week of serving. And that is so impactful, because serving for a week is exhausting, but it's one of the best things I have ever experienced!"

– Kailyn J., Missionary

CHAPTER 12

An Extreme Opportunity to Serve:
Steve Butcher, Board Member

Steve Butcher's Barnabas journey began when he received a call in July 2005 from the producers of the former reality show *Extreme Makeover: Home Edition*. They asked if Steve, as the president of pb2 Companies, would like to be a contractor for an upcoming makeover in Purdy, Missouri.

Steve had provided architectural services and helped with construction for a makeover in Alma, Arkansas, the month before, so he understood the scope of the task: procuring the materials and labor needed for a home renovation completely through donations. For the Camp Barnabas project, the crew planned to renovate the Teas family's house, which was on Camp property, as well as two additional structures: the Silver Lining, an indoor game space for Campers, and the Barnabunk, a building that would house forty volunteers.

Despite the project's complexity, Steve quickly agreed to the task.

"I agreed [to the Barnabas project] because the [Alma] project was so challenging, and the bonds of friendship happen very quickly in such a situation. Besides marrying my wife and having kids, it was one of the greatest experiences of my life."

Steve traveled to Camp Barnabas with two of the producers, Conrad and Di, to check out the property and get a better understanding of the scope of the project. However, since the TV show typically began by surprising the homeowners, Steve and the producers had to visit Camp undercover in order to keep Paul and Cyndy Teas in the dark. The trio called ahead and asked for permission to come visit Camp as potential donors—which they were, Steve pointed out, just not in the way Camp Staff expected.

"I had no idea such a place existed, let alone close to where I had lived for forty-four years. Walking into Camp for the first time . . . I was pretty well stunned by what I saw," Steve said. "As I walked down the trail, Conrad said, 'This will be an Emmy.' He was right."

Before long, Paul Teas spotted them and came over to see what these three strangers were doing at Camp.

"Paul was a bit cautious and understandably protective. He was also determined to find out why we were there. We were not prepared for that, but keeping our agenda secret was an absolute necessity."

While trying to deflect Paul's questioning, Steve found himself drawn to—and almost overwhelmed by—all the activity at Camp.

"Wild-eyed kids and adults whizzing around with a kind of energy I had never seen before. A kind of pure joy. A sort of energy and love that resonated throughout the atmosphere."

After talking for a while, Paul agreed to give Steve, Conrad, and Di a tour of Camp, which allowed them to gather the information they needed to plan the show.

Purpose-Driven Work

With the "Door Knock" scheduled for August 17, 2005—the day when the show's crew would arrive at Camp and surprise Paul and Cyndy, the Campers, and the Staff with the message that they had been chosen—things began to move quickly. Steve; his wife, Yavonne; and his team at pb2 Companies began reaching out to the community to line up donations.

One obstacle quickly became obvious—Camp Barnabas was so remote that nearby hotel rooms were scarce. The team ended up building an RV park in a field on the south side of Camp— complete with water, sewer, and electric—so the crew could get a little rest before driving into town after long shifts that often lasted more than twenty-four hours.

Steve with his wife, Yavonne, and youngest daughter, Grace, just after turning over the keys to Ty Pennington for the Teas family's new home

The other obstacle had been known upfront: finding donors for all the materials and construction crews, as well as volunteers to support and feed the crews. Yavonne began making calls to people in the community. By the time the Door Knock arrived, pb2 had everything they needed to get started, including eighty-five pieces of heavy equipment, more than 6,000 planned meals, and approximately 500 skilled volunteers and 2,000 support volunteers.

On August 17, everyone gathered outside Paul and Cyndy's home. The family had been sequestered inside by a producer who told them they needed to wait for a phone call from ABC that would tell them whether they had been selected for the makeover. Outside, a large crowd of cast, crew, Campers, volunteers, and construction teams gathered.

"The crowd was completely quiet when Ty [used] his bullhorn to blast the news to [Paul and Cyndy] to come out," Steve remembered. "As the Teas family [exited] the home into a thunderous roar of excitement, a precious moment was created. One that can't be put into words—just a gift from God for everyone."

The Teas family was sent on vacation for a week, and the team got to work. The rest of the first day was used for staging and filming, while the second day was demolition day. The makeover team made the decision to burn Paul and Cyndy's emptied-out house to the ground in a symbolic representation of a camp bonfire. The massive bonfire created another unforgettable experience as Campers and crew members gathered around the burning house and listened to country singer Trisha Yearwood perform.

After that, 105 hours were left to complete all three buildings.

"Those 105 hours were filled with countless wonderful stories of encounters that bonded complete strangers together," Steve said. "It was all so purpose-driven. There were people that pushed themselves to the point of achieving more than they thought was possible. It was life-changing for many. Adults worked as if they were children playing—going beyond the point of exhaustion, because they didn't want to stop. They were in a state of purpose-driven flow because the feeling of God's presence was magnified by so much love and so much praying that the energy was irresistible."

One of the most special parts for Steve was getting to work together with his wife and four children. His wife worked with the meal volunteers, keeping food coming for the cast and crew, while his children helped however they could.

"The experiences were life-changing for our family. Watching my wife as she kept great meals coming out by the hundreds day and night, and carrying on with such joy working with the chefs and volunteers. Our oldest daughter, Jessica, helping her mom. Watching our son, Brandon, as a young man using his building skills to take on any task until he simply couldn't stand up and then laying on a piece of cardboard and falling asleep, exhausted and happy. Seeing our teenage daughter, Heather, find her calling to go to Camp every year as a [Missionary], ultimately becoming a behavioral analyst as an adult. Our seven-year-old daughter, Grace, running around, smiling all the while and engaging with all sorts. What a great blessing for a person to see loved ones so happy."

Steve also thoroughly enjoyed working with the *Extreme Makeover* cast and crew.

"They had a very specific purpose and scripting to execute their roles to make the production as professional as possible, which they did. But they are also people with big hearts and love what they do. Often, they were truly touched by moments that can never be forgotten."

At one point during the week, a producer asked a cast member to interview a young lady in a wheelchair. Steve was nearby and watched what unfolded. He noted that the Camper seemed very frail but was completely undaunted by attention from the cast and crew or the large camera pointed at her.

"After a little chitchat, the cast member asked the Camper what was causing her to be ill. [She] named some very complex medical term for her condition. She was then asked about her prognosis. In a completely happy and matter-of-fact way, she said, 'Oh, I have about one to two weeks to live. I want to spend as much of the time as possible here with my friends.' The cast and crew could not continue. They were broken. Her spirit and faith were overwhelming. The young lady was completely content, brave, and had no fear. She knew she was in God's hands and felt safe."

Lifelong Blessings

By the time the project ended, the team had completed all three buildings, as well as approximately an eighth of a mile of new pavement through Camp and

Burning down the Teas family's old home

Steve's wife, Yavonne, whom he credits as the unsung hero of *Extreme Makeover* because of her work feeding the cast and crew 24/7

an extensive network of underground utilities, including sewer, water, and electric.

The big reveal of the completed projects for the Teas family created another memorable moment.

"Ty [Pennington, the host] and the crowd yell 'Move that bus!' and the new home is revealed," Steve said. "The moment of the reveal is another one of those roaring moments that are forever etched in your mind. It is such a wonderful gift. I am grateful for the memory."

The episode of *Extreme Makeover: Home Edition* featuring Camp Barnabas and the Teas family aired on October 16, 2005. It would go on to be nominated for and win an Emmy for Outstanding Reality Program.

For Steve, the experience left a permanent mark on his life. He would go on to become a board member for Camp Barnabas and served as the board chairman for three years.

"Since day one, Barnabas has been a tremendous blessing for my family. Having any involvement in Barnabas is a gift to the giver. We certainly can't outgive God," Steve said. "In the seventeen years since I first walked into Barnabas, a few things have been made clearer to me. God's master plan is far beyond my comprehension. Most of the Campers have something that very few adults can claim—unconditional love for others, which is the ultimate Christ-like trait. It is a blessing to have the opportunity to serve at or donate to Camp Barnabas."

"Camp has helped me grow spiritually in my walk with God. Since my sister has special needs, it has helped me understand how much this week means to both the Campers and their families. I love serving at Camp and plan on serving every summer."

– Lucy J., Missionary

CHAPTER 13

The Joy of Welcome:
Libby Schaller, Parent

In 2005, Libby Schaller's family was preparing to move from Dallas, Texas, to northwest Arkansas, when an episode of *Extreme Makeover: Home Edition* about a camp in southwest Missouri started playing on their TV. Libby's son, Wade, said, "Hey, I think that's near where we're moving."

Sure enough, Camp Barnabas was only about fifty miles from the Schallers' new home, and their daughter, Emmy, was almost seven at the time—just the right age to start attending Camp.

"We had no idea that our relationship with Barnabas would last for so many years," Libby said. "When Emmy was born in 1998, we noticed rather quickly she was not developing at the same rate as her peers and as her brother had. After years of testing, she was diagnosed with an intellectual disability, and after much genetic testing, her disability does not have a known cause or diagnosis."

When Emmy was young, Libby was always looking for activities she could be involved in, because Emmy was happiest when she was with other people. Unfortunately, Libby found limited after-school programs and summer activities for a child whose chronological age does not match her developmental age.

Emmy and Wade at Camp together

"I just felt like whatever I could expose her to safely would be a good thing. Some are going to be better than others, but everything's worth a try."

So Libby signed Emmy up for Camp Barnabas, starting in the summer of 2006. The memories of opening day brought tears to her eyes as she recalled how the Missionaries greeted Emmy with joyful smiles, shouting her name as they welcomed her to Camp.

"Emmy was embraced and treated like a superstar for a full week," Libby said. "You would walk up to this gathering of young people jumping up and down screaming, and they all act like the greatest thing that's ever happened to them is that *Emmy* has just walked up. So they start screaming and yelling, and she loves it. . . . They hug her, and then her Counselor—her Missionary—kind of pops out of nowhere . . . and then they sweep her off to her cabin."

The next moments were surreal for Libby and her husband, Bart.

"You are left in the car by yourself, and someone has just willingly, with great joy and glee, taken your child. Normally, we're begging and pleading to be included," she explained. "We go to something like this for typical children and say, 'I don't want extra special treatment—we don't want to put you out. But can she come to your activity? I promise she won't be a burden.' That's usually the feeling of a parent of a child with special needs, but this time, they're like, 'Bring her on!' and off they go with her. That whole moment, you're thinking, 'Oh my goodness, these people love my child already.'"

Each year, Bart and Libby could tell that Emmy was having a wonderful time at Camp through photos posted on an app for parents and families and through notes from Missionaries that came home in her suitcase. Emmy wasn't able to articulate many stories from her time there, so they were even more excited when their son, Wade, attended Camp through the Sibling Program for two years. As a parent, Libby said, it was a joyful relief to know her two kids were there together and that Wade could keep an eye on Emmy.

"I have talked with other families over the years who are hesitant to let their child with special needs go away to spend the night somewhere without them," Libby said. "I assure them that Camp Barnabas is the greatest place. They are loved, they are encouraged, they have fun, and they feel special for five full days."

Emmy has continued to attend Camp Barnabas every summer, even now that she's a young adult. For many families, these five days provide a break that allows the parents to focus on their other children or on their marriage, or simply take a week of rest. For Libby and Bart, it was a chance to get away with Wade, doing things they might not do with Emmy along. Now that Wade is grown and married, Camp Barnabas still provides Libby and Bart with a chance to get away, even when they just stay at home that week.

"Camp Barnabas really changed our lives, one week at a time every summer," Libby continued. "You would enroll for the next summer right away and then plan your family vacation around that trip. It goes on the calendar, and you don't do anything that would jeopardize that week."

Joining Barnabas Prep

For many parents, the first seventeen or so years of raising a child follow a predictable script: school, after-school and summer activities, family trips, and so on. When the road forks at the end of high school, parents help their kids navigate their next steps. But for any parent of a child with a disability, the end of high school looms large. The number of programs available for people with disabilities decreases drastically after they finish high school.

"We refer to it amongst my friends that it feels like we're falling off a cliff when they get into high school, because you worry what's next?" Libby explained. "I have no idea. There's really not much for adults. As a parent, it's a scary time. The other terrifying thought for any parent of a child with a disability is, 'What will happen to my child if something happens to me?' We are all encouraged to keep current with our wills and establish a special needs trust."

With that question always in the back of her mind, Libby started researching a wide variety of residential programs located everywhere from New York to Tennessee.

"We just needed a plan for if something happened, so we could tell my son, 'This is what we have set up for now.'"

Though she still has other residential programs she plans to check out, she found one that she loves, which brought some peace of mind. Next, Libby began looking for college-like opportunities.

Bart and Libby dropping Emmy off at Barnabas Prep

And there was Barnabas Prep right in their backyard.

Barnabas Prep, a Christian collegiate program designed to help young adults with disabilities achieve high levels of independence, was founded in 2011 as a sister ministry to Camp Barnabas. Libby had heard about Barnabas Prep at Camp around the time Emmy was fourteen or fifteen. When she heard about it again the next year, she wrote a deposit check right then and there.

"I don't know when we'll be here, but save my spot," she said.

When Emmy was old enough to attend, Libby and Bart went to visit Prep and discovered that it was just right for Emmy, with its small size and an emphasis on teaching life skills and social skills.

"Barnabas Prep stepped in and said, 'We will be next,'" Libby explained. "'We will teach her the next steps of how to do laundry, hold meaningful conversation, pick out appropriate clothes, interact with friends on a daily basis, and even practice some job skills on campus and in the community. Of course, Bart and I have been teaching Emmy those skills too, but we all know we are a little more dependent when Mom and Dad are around. Prep has high expectations for Emmy, and they hold her accountable, which leads to amazing growth each year."

Emmy has been attending Prep for three years now and loves it.

"Barnabas Prep has just been huge for all of us," Libby said. "I can't say enough wonderful things about it!"

Part of the Solution

The list of challenges for people with disabilities and their families is long, but Libby, who joined the board of Barnabas in 2022, is grateful for the resources she has and the ones she has found through Barnabas, which make life a little easier. She knows that many other families have a hard time finding the support they need.

"Finding caregivers or after-school programs that will welcome children or adults with disabilities is quite difficult," she said. "Then you consider the cost of long-term care for adults with disabilities, and for many families, it's not an option. As these families are trying [to provide for themselves], they never imagined they would have to afford a whole lifetime for someone else."

She doesn't know what the answer is to all those challenges, but for her family, Barnabas Prep has provided part of the solution.

"Prep is not year-round, but it does allow us some time to be adults and to figure out what we are going to do when we do need a full-time residential solution for Emmy."

From the full-time Staff to the Prep Fellows to the volunteers, Libby is continually amazed by the people at Barnabas, and she's grateful for the warm welcome they extend to families like hers.

"These fabulous Missionaries at Camp and the Fellows at Prep . . . every time I think, 'Where did you come from?' Here they are, this whole Camp or school full of all these people who see these children as equals and made in

Emmy in the lake at Camp Barnabas, Summer 2022

Libby and Emmy at Prep

God's image," she continued. "We need to be celebrating these people who give up their time and their talent to come to Camp and Prep and give back, because it is not an easy job."

She recalled a meeting at Emmy's high school where the assistant principal asked Libby and Bart if they knew how hard it was for the school to find people to work with kids like Emmy.

"We were just taken aback at the burden our daughter had seemingly put on the school system," Libby remembered. "So that's just how it feels. You feel like you're always, always fighting for your child."

She smiled. "And then Barnabas is fighting to have your child come. They call, and they ask: 'Do you need scholarship money? Do you want to come another time? Is there anything else we can do for you?' It is just so overwhelming to be so wanted. It doesn't feel natural, which is really unfortunate, but it's much appreciated."

Libby views Barnabas Camp and Barnabas Prep as embodiments of God's Word.

"Barnabas celebrates, teaches, and encourages people with disabilities and the neurodiverse, treating them with the respect and love deserved by all," she said. "What a gift, what a joy to be welcomed!"

"Camp always brings joy to my heart, because my limp due to cerebral palsy is 'normal' at Camp. ... [Going to Camp means] one week of unconditional love where people see the limp but look back up and smile at me. That doesn't happen outside [Camp's] gates."

– Shannon S., Cabin Parent

CHAPTER 14

The True Gift Is Your Heart:
Rhonda Francka, Camper

Rhonda Francka is a poet. An encourager. An advocate. Ask any number of people at Camp Barnabas, and they'll have a story to tell about something Rhonda said or did that has impacted them.

On her first birthday, Rhonda was diagnosed with cerebral palsy. The doctor predicted Rhonda would be walking within six months, but she would have seizures and significant intellectual disabilities. He advised her parents to put her in a home.

They replied with a firm no.

"The good Lord blessed us with her," they told him. "We're not putting her in a home."

As it turned out, the doctor was wrong on every single point. Rhonda has never walked, but she has also never had seizures and has no intellectual disabilities. Today, as an adult, Rhonda uses a wheelchair and relies on help from her family and caregivers, but she is grateful for all that she is able to do.

New Opportunities and Faithful Friends

Throughout most of each year, Rhonda enjoys keeping in touch with friends from around the country, writing poetry, and exploring other creative outlets like learning to make candles. But without a doubt, her favorite week of the year is spent at Camp Barnabas.

She first heard about Camp Barnabas while watching an episode of *Extreme Makeover: Home Edition* that featured the Camp.

"I saw people just like me," she said.

Though she was already an adult at the time, she called Camp Barnabas to see if they had a week for her. Since Camp doesn't have any age restrictions for its Campers, the answer was an enthusiastic yes. They sent her an application by mail, and she was accepted for the following summer.

During her first week at Camp in 2006, Rhonda vividly remembers her cabin's first activity: ziplining.

"I was the first one up," she said with pride. "One of my Cabin Staff was up at the top doing the ropes course. And she goes, 'One, two—bye!' I loved it. That's my favorite activity."

She remembers lying in bed that first night, too excited to sleep.

"I'm lying there, and all the sudden we hear the Missionaries screaming, and they all run in and start dumping everybody's suitcases in the middle of the floor. I'm like, 'What the heck are you guys doing?' And they're like, 'We think a skunk got in the cabin.'" She laughed at the memory.

The alleged skunk never made another appearance, but the night's chaos was still evident the next morning.

"All the suitcases were dumped out in the middle of the floor, so they had to sort people's clothes out before we could even get dressed." Rhonda grinned.

There are a dozen other stories Rhonda could tell about funny things that have happened at Camp—that time they spent the night in a treehouse and her Counselors got lost in the woods trying to find the restroom in the middle of the night, or the time she and her Counselor had to race to beat a thunderstorm—"because rain and power wheelchairs do not mix."

Rhonda also loves that Barnabas is a place where the answer is always "yes."

"I've gotten to ride horses, which I never thought I would get to do," she said. "I got to do paintball. One year we got to do laser tag. . . . It's just so much fun."

Although the activities and funny stories are memorable, they don't compare to the meaningfulness of the relationships she has made through Barnabas.

"I always say, 'You can't take the activities home with you, but you can take the friendships.' So when I'm at Camp, I work on my friendships, because those will last if you take care of them."

Rhonda always attends Week Four of Camp Barnabas, a week for Campers with physical disabilities. For her, it's a time of catching up with friends from across the country, specifically the group of women she shares a cabin with every year.

"We all just love each other. That's our group. They don't really try to split us up. They've tried, but it doesn't work." Rhonda smiled. "We come to Camp to see each other—our friendships are more important than the activities. And I don't get to go see these people [all the time] . . . they're all over the United States. In that one week, we get to hang out, and it's so awesome."

After more than fifteen years attending Camp, Rhonda has also created strong bonds with several Missionaries and Staff Members who have seen her through some hard times.

When Rhonda's mom passed away in 2013, two Barnabas Staff Members in particular went the extra mile to make sure Rhonda felt loved and cared for during that time.

"Back then, Sarah Wilson was the missionary director," Rhonda said. "Sarah's one of my best friends. . . . When we were told my mom was brain dead, Sarah stayed up till 2:30 in the morning texting with me."

Rhonda at Camp, Summer 2023

A couple months after Rhonda's mom passed away, Sarah, along with Alison Brawner, wife of then-CEO Jason Brawner, and Alison's two kids drove to see Rhonda and spend the day with her.

"They didn't have to, but they did it anyway," she said. "[Barnabas Staff and Missionaries have] helped me get through some really tough, tough times."

Advocating for Change

Rhonda wishes more organizations would focus on educating individuals with disabilities about the services available to them. She knows firsthand what a difference the right resources can make, and she's passionate about spreading the word.

For many years, Rhonda used Medicaid to hire a caregiver, but she found that limited her options. For example, her caregivers through Medicaid weren't allowed to take her to the doctor, let alone take her shopping or out to a movie. Rhonda's father typically took her to doctor's appointments, but as he aged, she began to worry about what would happen when he passed away someday.

A couple years ago, she learned that she qualified for a waiver from the government that would cover care for eight hours per day. That daytime care has provided many new opportunities for her.

"Through my waiver, I can have my caregiver take me to the doctor. We can go out to eat, we can make crafts. . . . I'm learning to make candles. Tomorrow, I get to go to the pumpkin patch with my favorite four-year-old," she said. "It's opened up my life . . . I have more control over my own life, which is amazing."

Rhonda also cares deeply about helping people understand some of the challenges of living with a disability.

Rhonda (second from left) at Camp, Summer 2023

One simple change Rhonda says would make a big difference is for doctor's offices to have lifts to help patients transfer from their wheelchairs. For example, when she went to get her wisdom teeth out, the office staff asked if she could transfer from her wheelchair to their chair by herself. When she told them she couldn't, they said they couldn't help her.

"I've had to go to the emergency room for things that I should be able to go to my primary care doctor for."

The other biggest change she would love to see is for people to make fewer assumptions about her disability. Over the years, she has had people shout at her or try to sign to her because they assume she can't hear them. She even had one woman pat her on the head.

"Or sometimes, when I go to the doctor, they try to talk to whoever I'm with instead of talking to me. And the person will have to say, 'She can answer your question,'" Rhonda said. "I wish people would understand that just because somebody has a harness on to help them sit up doesn't mean that they're deaf or that they [have a developmental disability]."

What Matters Most

Rhonda loves inspiring others with disabilities, especially through her poetry. Through it, she celebrates people's differences but also encourages people with disabilities to hold themselves accountable for their own behavior.

When Rhonda was two years old, her parents took her to a preschool for children with disabilities. At one point, the preschool's director pulled her parents aside to give them some advice.

"You need to treat her just like you would any of your other children," the director said. "If she needs to be disciplined, you need to discipline her just the same, because she's going to need help all her life, and people won't want to help her if she's a spoiled brat."

"That was the best advice they could have gotten," Rhonda said. "I've seen so many people with disabilities think the world owes them something, who will take their chairs if they get mad and run into people. That's not acceptable."

One year at Camp, Rhonda asked the Staff if she could read one of her poems at Wrap Up—the Camp-wide gathering at the end of each day.

"I'd been trying to get it right for three years," she remembered. "And I finally got it right."

At first, the Staff told her there wouldn't be an opportunity for her to read the poem at Wrap Up, but she could read it during Rally, the time right after lunch when Campers can take the microphone and get each other hyped up. But since only half the Campers would be present at Rally, Rhonda wasn't convinced.

"I really feel like all the Campers and all the Staff need to hear this," she told one Staff Member.

When the Staff Member held firm on his decision, Rhonda agreed to read her poem at Rally. Afterward, the same Staff Member approached her.

"I was wrong," he said. "You were right. Everybody does need to hear this."

Then he asked Rhonda to come back the next day to read her poem to the other half of Camp.

"I'm always trying to encourage, because I want people to know their outside body is just a wrapping paper. What matters is your heart. It's OK if you're frustrated that you have a disability, but you shouldn't use your disability to get what you want. You shouldn't use your disability as an excuse for bad behavior, because God's going to look at your heart, and He's not going to take excuses."

True Gift

I use a wheelchair as my legs,
That is just my wrapping paper,
don't be afraid to look inside
because the true gift is my heart!

I may be non-verbal, or my speech might not be clear,
That is just my wrapping paper,
don't be afraid to look inside
because the true gift is my heart!

I may use sign language because I can't hear,
That is just my wrapping paper,
don't be afraid to look inside
because the true gift is my heart!

I might process the world differently,
That is just my wrapping paper,
don't be afraid to look inside
because the true gift is my heart!

By Rhonda Francka
May 16, 2022

"I was really scared at first because I'd never really been away from home.

"But yeah, I loved it though."

– Mallory S., Camper

CHAPTER 15

An Invitation to Community:
Carley McGovern, Camper

Though Carley McGovern grew up with cerebral palsy, she never really interacted with other people with disabilities until she went to Camp Barnabas for the first time in 2007 at age twenty-one. Carley attended a private high school, and for fun, she joined in on whatever her brothers were doing.

"My family just does whatever. I didn't have any special things I did, other than therapy and stuff like that," she said. "I'd been around some [people with disabilities] . . . but it wasn't something I looked for. . . . Even though I had a disability, I wasn't aware that I needed similar people like me."

In 2005, some friends of her parents watched the *Extreme Makeover: Home Edition* episode about Camp Barnabas. Touched by the story, they signed up to volunteer at Camp the next summer. When they got back, they couldn't say enough good things about their experience, and they urged Carley to go.

"I was like, 'Are you sure I should go? I don't want to go hang out in the middle of the woods with people I don't know—that seems a little weird.'"

But her friends assured her she would love it.

Still unconvinced, Carley decided to watch the *Extreme Makeover* episode. "After that, I was like, 'All right. Sign me up, Mom. I have to go.'"

Though Carley was curious to see what Camp Barnabas was like, traveling from her home in Maryland to southwest Missouri for a week at a Camp where she didn't know anyone was still a little nerve-racking.

Despite her nerves, it took Carley very little time to realize she'd made a good decision.

"I was like, 'Oh my God, this place is amazing,'" she remembered. "I was there for three hours, and I was like, 'I am never going to leave this place ever again.'"

Since that first summer, Carley has tried to recruit others to come with her and experience what she did.

"After that first year, I convinced my parents to go with me as Cabin Parents . . . so they went, and my brothers volunteered too, so that was really fun," she

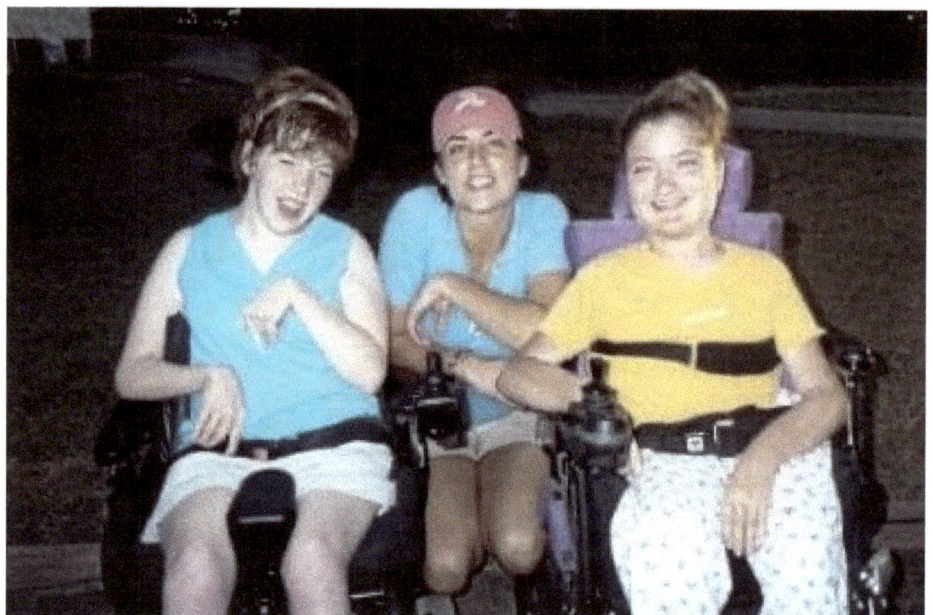
Carley (left) and her friend Mallory at Camp Barnabas

said. "I didn't shut up about it for the entire year, so they were like, 'OK, I guess we have to go.'" She laughed.

Friends and Fellowship

By far, Carley's favorite thing about Camp was the tight-knit community and the opportunity to build new friendships.

"I just loved the whole community feel of it," she explained. "There's nothing else like it. It's just like a big family basically. . . . It's amazing the way you see God work there through the people and the connections you'll have for years after."

During her first week at Camp, Carley met Mallory Stone, who would become a life-long friend.

"The funny thing is she wasn't supposed to be there that week," Carley remembered.

Mallory had already completed her volunteer week as a Missionary Partner by the time Carley came to Camp, but she found herself bored at home. So she called Cyndy Teas and asked if there were any spots left for her to return as a Camper. Amazingly, there were, and Mallory and Carley ended up in the same cabin. In the years to come, they would also become friends with Rhonda Francka,[1] Lorie Sparks,[2] and several other women who have formed a tight-knit community.

---

[1] Rhonda's story can be read in Chapter 14.

[2] Lorie's story can be read in Chapter 18.

"I feel like most of us don't care about the activities anymore," Carley said. "I mean, they're super fun and they're great for people who like them, but for us it's just a family reunion basically."

Moments of fun and connection with friends are what stand out most in Carley's memories of Camp.

"It's stupid stuff like getting to brush your teeth together with your best friend . . . or getting to sleep over with your friend in the same cabin and even the late-night talks."

She loves Wrap Up each evening because everyone at Camp attends, and it gives her the opportunity to see friends who aren't in her cabin. Devotional times with her cabin are another favorite.

"Each summer has a theme, and [the Staff] finds verses that go along with the theme, and we just discuss them. But with our group, it usually turns into [talking about] what we're going through based on the Scripture. It's really fun just to see how God's working in everyone's life. It's one of our favorite times."

Carley remembers being surprised at how close she grew to some of her Missionaries too.

"You wouldn't think after one week that you'd be super close with these people. But you do get super close to them. It's super weird, but it's super cool."

Since she lives far away from most of her Camp friends, keeping up can be hard at times, Carley said. But she does her best, talking frequently on the phone and visiting friends in person whenever she can.

"It's hard to be far away, but that's what FaceTiming is for, right?"

A New World

Camp Barnabas has helped Carley grow in ways she never expected, including in her faith.

"I'd say I grew up in a Christian home. But after [Camp], my faith became my own thing and not something I was forced to do," she said. "My personal relationship with Jesus grew beyond just something our family did. It was more like me choosing to do it."

One of the biggest ways Camp Barnabas changed Carley's life was through introducing her to more people with disabilities and giving her the opportunity to build friendships with them.

"This is gonna sound really weird, but [before coming to Camp Barnabas,] I was scared of people with disabilities, even though I had one. I guess it comes from not being around them a lot," she explained. "[Before Camp] I felt like the world of disability to me [was] closed, and then it opened up. I was like, 'Wow!' Like, I can't survive my life anymore without people with disabilities in it."

Today, Carley is involved in the disability community in a variety of ways. Her parents split their time between Florida and Maryland, so when she's in Florida with them, she participates in Young Life's ministry to people with disabilities called Capernaum. When she's in Maryland, she works at Bitty & Beau's

Coffee, a coffee shop run by people with disabilities. She is also involved with a camp called Hope Heals that offers retreats for individuals with disabilities and their families.

All of that involvement and the community she's come to find was first sparked by Camp Barnabas.

"I'm so grateful for Camp and so grateful that Paul and Cyndy had it in their hearts to [create] a camp [where] I feel belonging, because that was really the first place I felt [that]."

An important memory from one Wrap Up during her first week at Camp comes to mind.

"I just remember looking around, being like, 'Wow, they created all this for *me*? What the heck?' Not just for me, but for all the Campers honestly. But I was so blessed to even be there. It's an awesome place."

To any potential Campers who might be apprehensive about trying Camp Barnabas like she was initially, Carley has a simple encouragement.

"Give it a chance," she said. "It will change you in ways you don't even realize it's going to."

"Experiencing Camp with my husband was one of the greatest blessings of our marriage so far. I was completely blown away by the absolute joy and presence of the Holy Spirit that filled every corner of Camp Barnabas."

– Madison W., Missionary

CHAPTER 16

An Unshakable Experience:
Jake and Whitney Hornberger, Missionaries and Summer Staff

Jake Hornberger and Whitney Reid were both teenagers the first time they volunteered at Camp Barnabas in 2008. For fifteen-year-old Whitney, volunteering was a chance to check off her "good deed" for the summer. For fourteen-year-old Jake, it was something he did to appease his parents. Neither had any idea of the life change they were about to experience.

Whitney describes her teenage self as someone who liked control, who always wanted to prepare for any difficult situation. Some of her friends had served at Camp Barnabas before, so she asked them what to expect, and they said she would probably need to help her Camper with eating, going to the bathroom, and other daily tasks.

"So I prepared myself for those things," she said. "And I was like, 'OK, I'm ready.'"

But when Whitney showed up to Camp, she was assigned to a Siblings' cabin. Camp Barnabas's Sibling Program encourages siblings of people with disabilities to attend Camp as well. Siblings stay in their own cabins and get the opportunity to connect with other kids who have similar experiences as their families.

Most of the girls in Whitney's cabin were only a year or two younger than she was, and since they were siblings of people with disabilities, Whitney reasoned that they already had more life experience than she did. It took no time at all for her to realize how unprepared she was.

Whitney pestered her Cabin Staff for advice. She laughed at the memory. "Bless those two Staffers that first year they had me, because I'm sure they were like, 'Oh, this girl is a mess.'"

But the Staff Members were kind in their encouragement. "Just come alongside them. Be a spiritual leader to them. Share wisdom and listen to them."

The problem was that Whitney knew in her heart she didn't have any spiritual wisdom to share.

"I was active in my youth group, but I wasn't really a believer," she explained. "I wanted to be a good person, and I was like, 'Oh, it would be so nice if

God was real and Jesus was real,' and all this stuff, but I had just kind of discarded it as, 'Oh, I don't think that's real. I think it's just something people like to tell themselves.' I was just kind of hard-hearted to the message of the gospel."

But during that week at Camp Barnabas, Whitney began to pray in earnest, perhaps for the first time in her life. "Help me, help me, help me, help me" became her constant plea.

"That week really broke me because I had nothing—I couldn't lean on myself at all. However, I kept going, and I felt like there were times where the Lord just truly spoke through me. Like I did not have the words to say, but my mouth opened, and some correct words came out. I just knew that that was a miracle—nothing from me, but from the Lord."

Near the end of that week, more aware of her own weaknesses than ever before, Whitney surrendered her life to Jesus.

"Lord, somehow, I feel You've been working through me," she prayed that night. "I know it's not me. This is the most true thing I've ever known. I've been running from You for so long. I've been so adamant in my denial that You even exist, and here I am asking for help. . . . God, I give up. I give up striving so hard, I give up this plan that I had for my life, because it is so ridiculous compared to the plan that I know that You have for me."

For Whitney, the important question isn't what led her to Camp Barnabas, but what led her back.

"There's a lot of things in life that you go, you do it, you come home, and you move on. But [Camp Barnabas was] an experience that I couldn't shake," she explained. "Before I even left the gates of Camp, I knew I would be back. I knew that this place was so special to my heart."

And she has come back, every summer, for fifteen years now.

A New Level of Responsibility

Jake describes himself as the opposite of Whitney in high school.

"I was extremely rebellious as a high school kid. Whitney was the goody two-shoes, and I was whatever the opposite of that is."

Looking back, Jake can see how much he craved freedom and responsibility as a teenager, but he didn't have many opportunities to pursue those desires in a healthy way.

The summer before his freshman year, his parents brought up the idea of serving at Camp Barnabas.

"Absolutely not," was Jake's first response. "That does not sound fun."

But they were adamant, so Jake eventually agreed to go.

"And for the first time, I had an extremely healthy and impactful way to exercise those cravings and desires in the form of being a Missionary," he said. "Freedom to make decisions that impacted the people around me in a positive way . . . and the responsibility of literally having another human life that you're responsible for—for feeding, bathing, and just generally having fun with. It puts that pressure on to perform in a way that was positive."

Even though he enjoyed the autonomy, Jake quickly realized how little he knew about taking on that level of responsibility.

"I had [the realization that] becoming a man doesn't mean doing all this on my own, but you have to have the humility to recognize that you don't have the power to love unconditionally . . . and perform perfectly all the time. It totally broke me, just brought me to my knees for the first time in my entire life in just this recognition of total depravity."

That experience led to a journey of ongoing refinement that has continued ever since.

A Barna-Match

Jake continued to volunteer at Camp every summer, but he and Whitney didn't meet until 2012 when they both worked as Summer Staff for the first time. They were assigned to a work project at the Shirt Shack together and became friends. Though neither of them came to Barnabas expecting to meet their future spouse, they admit Camp Barnabas is a great place to meet someone because so much of the vetting process has already been done.

"Going into it, I knew immediately that she was a believer," Jake said. "I knew that she had devotion to selfless service and a passion for dying to herself for the sake of those around her. I was able to watch from a distance and see her ability to lead other girls and women. And I was able to see [that she was] going to be an awesome mom someday. Whoever ended up with her was going to be super lucky. And then on top of that, she just happened to be the prettiest girl at Camp."

Jake and Whitney's engagement at Inspiration Point at Camp Barnabas

Whitney laughed at his statement. "I don't know. I showed up in socks and Chacos. Before he and a couple of his buddies knew my name, they were just like, 'Oh, that girl in the socks and Chacos.' They called me 'sockos' for the first couple days."

Jake didn't think he had a shot at more than friendship, but he and Whitney stayed in touch after returning to college the next fall—Whitney to Auburn and Jake to Texas A&M. Then he surprised her by visiting her for her birthday and confessed he was interested in more than friendship. They began dating and continued their long-distance relationship for three years until Whitney moved to College Station, Texas, to begin nursing school at A&M.

Jake and Whitney got engaged at Inspiration Point at Camp Barnabas and then were married in 2017 by the CEO of Barnabas at the time, Jason Brawner, with many groomsmen and bridesmaids who were friends from Camp. Together, they've continued to serve each summer at Barnabas, Whitney as a nurse and Jake as a small group leader for high school students from their home church in Dallas.

Lasting Impact

Both Jake and Whitney have continued to be impacted by their time at Camp Barnabas in profound ways. For Whitney, a ton of Campers have become good friends. Additionally, her career path was dramatically affected by her time at Camp Barnabas.

As someone diagnosed with Crohn's disease at age twelve, Whitney knew what it was like to be "the sick kid."

"I think that that experience definitely helped me relate more on a heart level, an empathetic level, in a very small way, with the Campers."

After her first life-changing summer at Camp Barnabas, Whitney started to consider what God was calling her to. The answer soon became clear: She wanted to serve people who were sick, especially those who needed extra care.

"Ever since then I was like, 'That's what I'm doing.' I never looked back. I knew."

Her major at Auburn was rehabilitation and disability services, which she loved. For a while, she considered going into physical or occupational therapy, but through her experiences watching nurses serve at Camp Barnabas and shadowing nurses as part of her degree, she was drawn to nursing instead.

"I realized that that was just a really great path for me to take, like a good label to put on this calling, that would continue to push that skill set forward, to keep being faithful in that."

Jake, meanwhile, keeps a picture of a Camper he cannot forget on his desk next to photos of his family.

Her name was Bethany. She had been diagnosed at age eight with MELAS, a disease primarily affecting the nervous system and muscles. Even before Jake encountered her at Camp, he'd heard about her contagious smile and desire to share about Jesus with everyone she met.

Jake and Bethany

By the time Jake met Bethany, her physical health had declined significantly. She used a wheelchair and was no longer able to speak. Jake noticed her spending a lot of time in the Well House that week and heard she'd had multiple seizures. He decided to try and hang out with her as much as possible.

"[The Staff] kept telling us that [MELAS] doesn't affect her brain, that she can hear and understand . . . so I'd go and walk with her and just kind of talk to her as if she was listening, and [I] didn't get much response or anything like that."

On the last night of Camp, all the Campers and Staff dressed up and went to a prom-themed Wrap Up party. Jake decided to make it a memorable night for Bethany.

"I went out and got a bouquet of wildflowers and put it together, wore a shirt with a collar, and stuff like that, and went out. She was in her dress coming up, and so I bent down and gave her the flowers and told her I wanted to dance with her.

"She immediately just beamed, this like massive smile. Someone got a picture of it, and I keep it on my desk all the time, because it was just super impactful. There was something there, and she was paying attention and listening and appreciated the conversations that we were having. So we went to the dance together, and we were dancing, she was smiling, and it was just an awesome time."

Four months later, Bethany passed away.

"I'll never forget the smile that she had," Jake said. "Being able to give her an awesome night and put a smile on her face . . . I'm sure that it was fun for her. But for me, it was some of the most fun I've ever had and [one of] the most impactful and heartwarming experiences that I've ever been given. Even in that state, she was still showing the love of Jesus and impacting people, and [she] did that all the way up until the day she died."

The Hands and Feet of Christ

Jake and Whitney agree that they've been irrevocably changed by their experiences at Barnabas.

As a small group leader for high school students, Jake has seen many other lives changed the same way his was through Camp Barnabas.

"There's something about being given that opportunity and working with that specific population of people . . . that you can't help but be changed by," he explained. "We live in an 'it's all about me' world. That mindset's ingrained at a very early age in America. But Camp Barnabas gives kids an opportunity to experience the alternative and see firsthand how that can be life changing going forward."

Whitney loves how people pour into each other at Camp. During a Med Staff devotional time in 2022, one of the nurses said, "I look around at Camp buzzing, and I just think, 'This is the church at its best.' You know what I mean?"

"I was like, 'Yes, absolutely,'" Whitney recalled. "That's exactly how we feel, because everybody's just out there being the hands and feet of Christ to each other and making disciples. Each person is trying to pour into the other person, helping them grow spiritually. It's just a beautiful thing to see."

Jake and Whitney have been involved with other organizations off and on over the years, but Barnabas has been a constant—one that they don't see changing any time soon. Even the arrival of their baby son, Everett, in early 2023 didn't

The Hornberger Family at Camp in 2023

keep them from serving at Camp that summer. Instead, they brought Everett along and served together as a family.

"One thing that's been super consistent in both of our lives has been Camp Barnabas and that passion," Jake said. "Maybe it's because both of our lives were completely flipped upside down and changed through that, but it's been a constant in our lives."

"It's hard to shake those people." Whitney smiled. "They just get in your life, and they love you so well. You just—you can't shake them."

"Camp Barnabas is simply JOY. It is a place that not only Campers look forward to all year long, but Missionaries, Barnstormers, and Cabin Parents as well."

– Stephanie B., Cabin Parent

CHAPTER 17

Respite for the Whole Family:
Becky Korasick, Parent

When Becky Korasick shares her family's story, it's hard to separate their experiences from Camp Barnabas.

Their oldest son, Micah, developed cerebral palsy after a severe illness when he was two weeks old and has been attending Camp since he was eleven. Their daughter, Kate, has attended Camp as a Sibling, Barnstormer, Missionary, and Staff Member, and their middle son, Joe, has been a Sibling, Barnstormer, and Missionary. As Missionaries, both Kate and Joe went through the Apostles Program as well. The Korasicks' youngest son, Conan, whom they adopted when he was three and who also has some disabilities, has been a Camper since he was seven. And though Becky and her husband, Todd, typically use the week their kids are at Camp to take a vacation and rest, one year they decided to serve as Cabin Parents.

"That really just increased our love of Camp as we were able to be there with [our kids]," Becky said. "That's not always the case when you see behind the scenes, but it definitely is at Camp. The more we saw, the more we fell in love with the program and the way it's intentionally designed to pour into not just the Campers but all the people who are serving there as well."

Their first year sending Micah to Camp Barnabas, Becky wasn't sure what to expect.

"I was really pretty scared to death to leave Micah for that long."

Though Micah can communicate his needs, Becky worried about whether his Missionary would be able to understand him or care for his physical needs. But when they met Micah's Missionary, her fears were relieved.

"The guy who was there to take care of him was like six-foot-five, this big burly guy from Alaska, whom God had totally sent to just love on our kid for the week."

For Micah, the activities at Camp are never as exciting or important as the friendships he's able to make.

Micah, Todd, Joe, and Kate at Camp Barnabas in

"One of the highlights of Camp every year has been the bond that he makes with his Missionary," Becky explained. "They really poured into him, and without fail, they've shared their stories with him as well."

When Kate first attended Camp Barnabas as a Sibling, she went reluctantly. Becky laughed, remembering the two letters they received from Kate that week—the first complaining and talking about how much she missed them and the second with only positive things to say. Joe loved the Sibling Program from the beginning and spent his time finding trees to climb, canoes to ride in, and fascinating new friends in the form of tarantulas.

"I just couldn't say enough good things about [the Sibling Program]," Becky said. "I think [Kate and Joe] felt at some point that it was almost sacrilegious to say, 'This is hard,' to be the sibling of someone who has pretty severe limitations on what they can do physically."

The Sibling Program gave Kate and Joe a place where they could feel seen, heard, and understood. Becky emphasized how important it is for her kids to be able to be honest about the hard realities of everyday life in their family.

"Because they still love their brothers very much, but those real effects on their lives can take a toll at times."

When Becky thinks about Kate and Joe's experiences working at Camp Barnabas versus attending a traditional summer camp, she can't help but note how much more spiritual growth they experienced at Barnabas.

"[At the other camps] the focus was all on them," she said. "Being the hands and feet of Jesus at Barnabas for the week definitely helped their spiritual growth so much more than [a concert] on the beach with an up-and-coming Christian artist—which has its place. But when they're able to walk that out and when they're at the end of their rope . . . and they pray for those Campers and really are able to love on them . . . that can escalate spiritual growth [in a way that is] difficult to describe."

Called to Adopt

Even before Becky and Todd were married, Becky had the desire to adopt. She and Todd were on the same page, but after having three kids, Todd wasn't sure their family had the capacity to welcome another child. For a while, Becky plied him with pictures of kids needing adoption, but while praying one night, she realized she wanted unity with her husband more than she wanted to adopt. So she closed the tabs on her computer with photos of the kids.

About three months later, Todd came home from work and told Becky, "After the kids go to bed tonight, we need to talk."

Concerned, she pulled him into the bedroom and closed the door. "What's happening? Are we moving? Are you changing jobs?"

"I just can't read my Bible and pray without the overwhelming feeling that we need to adopt," he said.

That was the beginning of a long and winding road to finding Conan. Their journey began by pursuing adoption of an eleven-year-old girl living in a residential home for children and adults with disabilities. During their first visit to the home, three-year-old Conan attached himself to their family.

"We totally fell in love with him," Becky said.

At first, the Korasicks tried to see if they could adopt the girl and Conan, but because the children were not biologically related, this request was refused. Since they had started pursuing the girl first, the Korasicks decided to continue her adoption process first and hoped to adopt Conan later.

Then the owner of the residential home called them.

Joe and Becky at Camp in 2015

Micah and Conan at Camp, Summer 2015

"I'm not saying to say no to her, but can you please say yes to him first? He needs to be in a different environment than what we can offer him, and all her needs are being met here."

"So it was through much prayer and tears that we shifted gears at that point and said, 'OK, we will say yes to him first,'" Becky said.

They still intended to adopt the girl as well, but in the time that it took for them to adopt Conan, she was adopted by another wonderful family. The Korasicks still receive updates from her adopted family, and today they have no doubt that God had prepared them to adopt Conan.

Due to a traumatic brain injury, Conan had some paralysis on his left side, impaired vision in his left eye, and dealt with severe short-term memory issues. At the time of his adoption, Conan used a wheelchair and could say only one word, and the Korasicks were told he might never expand his vocabulary.

"Today, he doesn't need a wheelchair at all," Becky said. "His paralysis doesn't slow him down, and he talks nonstop. He's made tremendous progress."

Camp Barnabas is a highlight of the year for Conan, who is now fourteen.

"He loves everything about Camp," Becky said. "Most people there know his name. He's super friendly and loves, *loves* the whole experience of Camp and really would think that he is qualified to work there at this point."

Becky has witnessed the spiritual impact Camp has had on Conan as well. Though he normally struggles with short-term memory, Conan memorized a Bible verse during his first year at Camp that he can still recite now.

"It was like, wow. Just to have other people who are intentionally pouring that kind of truth and love into your kids for that week is invaluable."

Something New

In 2018, Becky and Todd began to feel strongly that God was preparing them for a change. They had been part of the same church in Illinois for twenty years, and Todd had eventually joined the staff.

"We just really felt like God was up to something new in our lives," Becky recalled. "We didn't know what that was, but it was just very clear that there was something else for us, and so we stepped away."

Transitioning was hard for everyone in their family, especially without knowing their next step. When a job opportunity in Idaho opened up for Todd, the Korasicks thought that was where God was leading. They bought a house, pulled their kids out of school, and had a going away party.

Two days before their moving date, however, Micah was hospitalized with a bad infection, and they canceled the moving truck. Shortly after that, they saw how God had been at work in preventing the move, as some previously undisclosed things came to light regarding the job in Idaho.

A few months later, a pastoral job popped up in Monett, Missouri—only a few miles from Camp Barnabas. Within a few weeks, Todd had an interview and was hired. And when they started house searching, the first home they looked at was already fully wheelchair accessible.

Becky remembers sitting in their van in front of the new house, tears streaming down her face, as she told the kids, "This is what it feels like when God has gone before you. He knew this was where we needed to be."

Being near Camp was an unexpected benefit. It allowed the Korasicks to continue seeing Kate on weekends when she worked at Camp for the summer, and since their home is fully accessible, they're able to host Campers at times as well.

"It's the coolest thing ever," Becky said.

Today, Todd and Conan hold down the fort in Monett, while Becky and Micah spend part of their week in Siloam Springs, Arkansas. There, Micah audits classes at John Brown University, and Becky works with Ability Tree, an organization that comes alongside families impacted by disability and equips the local church to welcome them.

Slowing Down and Trusting God

One of the biggest things Becky has learned from Micah, Conan, and other individuals with disabilities is the value of slowing down.

"[They're] not a burden to be cared for but [they] really add to this scope of humanity, when we can stop with so much pity and maybe add in more curiosity and really get to know the fun things about them," she explained. "But it requires us to slow down. I love that. By nature, I love to be productive, and so I feel that tension when I'm like 'OK, slow down.' The best way for me to connect with Conan is to play UNO and talk with him . . . but that requires me to stop all my stuff."

From Micah in particular, she has learned about patience and dependence on God.

"I don't know a more patient person in the world than Micah, because he has to be patient for every single drink that he ever gets, everything," she said. "His ultra-dependence on people, I think, actually makes it easier for him to understand how to be ultra-dependent on God. It's really just a beautiful thing."

Becky recalled a time when they took Micah to an intensive physical therapy program in California when he was young, and he began talking to his therapist, Justina, about Jesus.

"Justina, do you have Jesus in your heart?" he asked.

"I don't know what that means," she responded.

"Don't worry. My mom will tell you."

Becky laughed at the memory.

"It's like—OK, put me on the spot right there. Micah can break down walls, even spiritual barriers, with people like none of the rest of us can, and Conan has the same ability," she said. "For the rest of the time in California, [Justina] went to church with us . . . we just saw some really cool things happening. It changes your perspective, and you don't really keep asking 'why' to God, but just trusting Him with, 'Man, you must be up to something powerful through this.'"

Parenting children with disabilities means never getting time off. Becky says there are times when she does a good job taking care of herself, her health, and her spiritual walk, and then there are times when she is exhausted to the

Kate and Conan at Camper arrival, Summer 2023

Kate and Micah at Camp, Summer 2023

point of not being able to get up in the morning—and sometimes both of those feelings can happen within the same week.

For Becky and Todd, the week their kids attend Camp provides the deepest rest they get all year. Todd takes the week off from work, and they vacation nearby, spending their days hiking, talking, and napping.

"I think last year, we took two or three naps in the afternoon because we could, and it was really, really restful. That's priceless for us," she said. "I have an amazing husband, and so he's really good at communication already . . . but it gives us a yearly check-in time to ask, 'How are you doing with this? And what can we do to make this next year better?'"

Through everything, the Korasicks have learned to look first to Christ and His work in their lives.

"Christ has been the center of our lives, and we've tried to make that the center of our home, where it's not just something that we go and talk about on Sundays, but this is life for us. This is where we depend on Him for our strength."

> "Camp made me fully comprehend the meaning of the word joy. The joy of the Lord that I experienced during my stay was unlike anything that I have ever felt. Now that I understand just how incredible pure joy is, I cannot wait to find ways to show joy to others."
>
> – Nadia S., Missionary

CHAPTER 18

The Gift of Connection:
Lorie Sparks, Camper

For Lorie Sparks, Camp Barnabas has become a place of friendship, where she feels like she belongs and is accepted. The fellowship she feels there is a gift, especially since making friends hasn't always been easy.

"My doctor didn't diagnose me as deaf until I was four years old. I was also born with cerebral palsy," Lorie said. "I went to crippled children's nursery school. I was trying to learn how to walk on crutches and trying to learn how to hear and communicate. The teacher wouldn't let me use my sign language, mostly oral, [so I would] learn how to use my speech, which was very frustrating. My deaf and hearing friends couldn't understand what I was trying to say. They [would] rather use sign language to communicate with me."

Despite those early difficulties, Lorie was determined to press on and gain independence.

"When I was in high school, I had some struggles because of learning disabilities, but I kept trying, and with the help of tutors, I was able to eventually go to college and get a bachelor's degree. I decided to move out of my parents' house right out of high school into an independent living program. I was very thankful for the life coach teaching me to cook [and] budgeting and taking me places when I needed to."

Lorie started working a vo-tech (vocational-technical) job for the Marine Corps in high school and continued working there after she graduated. While she enjoyed the job, it kept her so busy that it left little time for friends. Eventually, loneliness crept in, and Lorie looked for other ways to get involved in the community and meet new people. She landed on theater as a good outlet.

"I wanted to get involved in theater and dance. I loved to act in the play and also take dance class. That was a joy for me," she said. "I can show [through] my passions for acting or dancing with a smile on my face that I can do all things that I put my mind to."

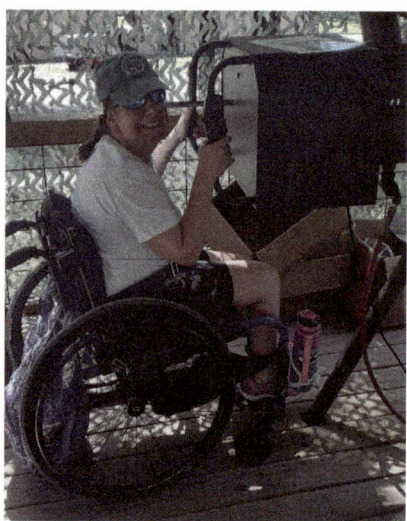

Lorie at Camp Barnabas

Growing in Faith and Friendships

Though finding friends wasn't always easy, one friend, Rhonda Francka,[1] has remained a steady presence in Lorie's life since they met through Girl Scouts at age eleven. Rhonda, who also has cerebral palsy, played a big role in Lorie's decision to attend Camp Barnabas.

When Lorie saw the *Extreme Makeover: Home Edition* episode about the Teas family and Camp, she became interested in attending. Initially, her mom discouraged her from applying, assuming that Lorie—who was in her thirties at the time—would be past Camp's age limit.

A few years later, Lorie and Rhonda scheduled a phone call to catch up. It had been a while since they talked, and Rhonda happened to mention that she'd been attending Camp Barnabas for several years. Since Lorie and Rhonda were the same age, Lorie and her mom thought, "Well, if Rhonda's going. . . ." Lorie applied and attended Camp for the first time in 2012 at age forty-two.

"I was very nervous and not expecting a lot of Staff and Missionaries jumping up and down excitedly," Lorie said. "My cabin was all nonverbal Campers, and [I] didn't make very many friends until one of the male Campers talked to me and welcomed me."

The first year, there was no interpreter available for Lorie, so communication and connecting with others was a little difficult. The next year, Lorie had an interpreter, which made all the difference in the world.

"It made me so happy I was able to chat with everyone," Lorie said. "The second year, I was able to make more friends."

Lorie loves the various activities at Camp from swimming, to ziplining, to the evening dance parties, to trying out the ropes course. Her first year trying

---

[1] Rhonda's story can be read in Chapter 14.

the ropes course, several of the Staff Members knew some sign language, which was a big help.

"The Staff . . . let me know what to do during the ropes course. They made me feel comfortable."

Lorie also enjoys connecting with Staff and Missionaries, teaching them and her other friends sign language and giving each of them a sign name.

"I really enjoyed hanging out with Staff and Missionaries. We can laugh and cheer each other up. My whole cabin would tease each other, and we would discuss [devotionals] with each other, help each other understand Bible study."

A few individuals stand out, including a Cabin Staff Member named Hailey whom Lorie assisted through the Missionary Partner (MP) Program; her Missionary Manda who knew sign language and helped Lorie be able to chat more freely with her friends; and Lorie's favorite Cabin Staff Member, Micayla, who always gave her hugs and made her feel loved and later invited Lorie to her wedding.

Lorie's favorite place at Camp is Inspiration Point, a beautiful area on a bluff overlooking the valley below, where Staff and Campers go for morning devotions.

"Our cabin really loves that place because you can look over the view. It's so pretty."

Through morning devotions, Bible study, and the friendships she's built at Camp, Lorie has seen her faith grow.

"I chose to be baptized there. I have learned a lot from the Bible studies. I pray every day right after I read the Bible . . . [and think over] what God has taught me while I am there."

A Place of Acceptance

The warmth and fellowship Lorie has experienced at Camp Barnabas is often, unfortunately, quite different from what she sees from the general public. She summarized a few of the things she'd love for people to do differently.

"When I go out in public, sometimes I need help pushing or opening a door and sometimes I don't. I appreciate when people ask if I want help and [don't] just ignore [me]. I can say yes or no. Also, just because I am short and in a wheelchair, I am not a child. I want to be included and treated like everyone else."

This makes the environment at Camp Barnabas all the more special. Lorie is grateful for the genuine acceptance that the Staff show to everyone who comes through the gates.

"The Camp Staff really want to serve God by serving all people, no matter their ability or challenges. I love seeing Missionaries wanting to help people and learn from seeing the different disabilities people have," she said. "I really appreciate how they accept everyone. It helped me accept who I am. I learned that [people with] all types of different disabilities can do all kinds of things. God made us very special."

Part 3

"Camp is a great reminder that God created each of us, and it is so important to treat each and every person in a way that dignifies who they are simply because they are a child of God."

– Sheila S., Cabin Parent

CHAPTER 19

Beautiful and Whole:
Sandy Miller, Director of Barnabas Prep

Nestled on twenty-two wooded acres just to the east of Lake Taneycomo in Branson, Missouri, Barnabas Prep is home to an average of forty Students and ten Fellows each year. Prep's mission is to equip young adults with disabilities for a life of self-confidence, societal significance, and spiritual maturity in Christ, and to help them achieve high levels of independence.

Barnabas Prep Students live in home-like dorms along with four to five Fellows—usually college-aged students who have taken a gap year to live and work at Prep. In addition to taking classes in job skills, fitness, and biblical studies, Prep Students also learn to do laundry, keep their rooms clean, and make simple meals. By living in community with each other and the Fellows, they also build their social skills.

Barnabas Prep was born out of Camp Barnabas in 2011 as Camp Staff became more aware of the lack of opportunities available for people with disabilities after high school. For the first two years, Barnabas Prep was housed at Camp Barnabas's main location in Purdy, Missouri. In 2014, Prep moved to its current location in Branson. At that time, all of Prep was housed in one large, yellow, Victorian-style house on the west side of campus. Since then, it has expanded to include two additional dorms, an office building with classrooms and a dining hall, a recreation center, and three small Intern houses for Students who are able to live on their own.

Life at Prep is always busy. A visitor walking through campus might find Students practicing a skit, learning to make applesauce, or watching a Bible-themed video. It's not a perfect place—some days find the Students sick with a flu bug or in tears over an interaction with another Student. But overall, it is a place of joy.

Sandy Miller, Barnabas Prep's director, has experienced this many times over.

"One thing that I've learned is you cannot come to Barnabas Prep and not be filled with joy. Because if you're coming and you're having a bad day—which everybody does—but you spend some time with [the Students], just that little old adage, 'Turn that frown upside down,' that's what happens here, because they love you. Period."

A Perfect Fit—Twice Over

As a parent to a thirty-year-old son who began attending Camp Barnabas at age seven, Sandy has been familiar with Barnabas for years. She still remembers the first time they sent their son, Justin, to Camp. They packed a disposable camera in his suitcase, and when he came home, it was full of pictures he'd taken with his Missionary.

"When we picked him up after the week was over, I was so glad to see him. But Justin was happy. He had a great time," Sandy remembered. "Right then, I was like, 'We made a good choice.'"

As Justin approached the end of high school, Sandy and her husband, Dave, considered the next step for their son. Justin never received an official diagnosis but is considered developmentally delayed. He was very active in high school and loved traveling with his school's football team as a team helper, so giving him a continued social outlet was important to Dave and Sandy. During high school, Justin had gotten involved with a local sheltered workshop—an organization that provides employment opportunities for people with disabilities. Since Justin's experiences with the sheltered workshop had been positive up until that point, it seemed like a good place for him to work after he graduated.

Unfortunately, that turned out not to be the case.

Justin at Camp

Justin at Camp

"[The other people there] were all older, and they were completely happy putting puzzles together," Sandy said. "If they were tired, they would just lay their heads down on the big long table and take a nap. They just weren't in his peer group, so it was not a good fit."

Sandy and Dave had heard about Barnabas Prep through Justin's time at Camp. Prep was just starting at the time, but after Justin's experience at the sheltered workshop, they knew they wanted to give Prep a try.

It ended up being the perfect fit. Since Sandy and Dave lived in Branson, they became close with many of the Prep Fellows, frequently hosting them for get-togethers. One of the Fellows even invited Justin and several other Students to be in her wedding when she got married.

"That was just such a sweet time, because Justin went from being very, very accepted in high school, to the sheltered workshop [not being] a good fit, to really learning and growing when he was at Barnabas Prep," Sandy said.

At the time, Sandy was an elementary school teacher. In passing, she once told her husband, "When I retire from teaching, I want to work for Barnabas. What a fun place to work."

Sandy retired in May 2016, in hopes of spending focused time with her family. But by that time, Justin had graduated from Barnabas Prep and moved into his own apartment in Branson, not far from Sandy and Dave. Their daughter, Allie, was attending Southwest Baptist University in Bolivar, Missouri.

"Nobody needed Mom anymore," Sandy said.

To prevent boredom, she found a job as the general manager of a mountain coaster in Branson—something she admits was not at all in her wheelhouse. Then in 2019, she ran into John Tillack, Barnabas's CEO,[1] after church. She had taught his children in school, so their families knew each other well.

"I wish you weren't still teaching," John told Sandy. "I need a director for Barnabas Prep."

"Well, John, I retired," Sandy said.

"Really? What are you doing now?"

"Running a mountain coaster."

"What?! You need to come talk to me."

After Sandy talked with John about the director position at Prep, Dave reminded her how she'd wanted to work for Barnabas one day. Everything seemed to line up just right. Sandy started her new role at the beginning of 2020.

However, things changed when the COVID-19 pandemic hit the U.S. in March, sending most of the country into lockdown. Many of the Barnabas Prep parents were willing to let their Students stay in the program—with Prep's isolat-

---

[1] John's story can be read in Chapter 26.

Students at Barnabas Prep

ed campus, the Staff and Students could easily quarantine there. But most of the Fellows' parents wanted their kids to come home.

"So we didn't have any Staff," Sandy said. "I'm like, 'OK, here I am, the director, with nobody to direct, no program.'"

She offered to step down, reasoning that she'd already retired once. But John and other Staff Members asked her to stay, confident that Prep's program would return. Eventually, it did.

"I love it. It's not like coming to work like at a job," she said. "You know, people are blessed when they have a career that they love, and I did that with teaching. Here, I get another one that I'm blessed [with]. That's very uncommon that you can have two careers you're passionate about."

A Safe Place to Learn and Grow

As the mom of a child with a disability, Sandy has a unique window into the experiences of Prep parents. She knows what it's like to feel like you're living on an island, without anyone who understands what it's like to parent children with disabilities. She has experienced the ache of having a child who missed out on many normal childhood experiences such as sleepovers, birthday parties, or prom. She understands the struggle to teach children with disabilities certain skills like tying shoes or doing laundry when, in the hustle of life, it's often easier for parents to do some of those tasks themselves.

That understanding builds a connection between her and prospective Barnabas Prep parents.

"[When I do tours,] for them to realize that they're not just talking to a person, they're talking to someone who has a Student with a disability, whose Student actually came to Barnabas Prep, and who is living a functional life outside of Prep now . . . it's not like [I] don't know what I'm talking about. I do know what it's like to have a kiddo with a disability. . . . And I know you don't always have time to teach them things because you're tired. I get that."

She's passionate about advocating for Students and seeking opportunities in the community for them to build their skills.

"In the world of COVID-19, I was telling people, 'You can't find help? Let me bring you some help.' Because [our Students] love to work and they love to serve . . . and they do it with such joy."

For many Barnabas Prep Students, their paycheck isn't nearly as exciting as the opportunity to do something they love. Mark, who loves learning about the Titanic, works in the gift shop at Branson's Titanic Museum. Hailey, stylish and driven, works three jobs: one at a salon, one at Vera Bradley, and one at Silver Dollar City. Cooper, brimming with enthusiasm for Barnabas Prep, says he wants to work there someday.

If Sandy could share one thing about Prep's Students, it would be how much the Students long to be part of the regular everyday routines that most people take for granted like going to work, having friends, and belonging to a community.

"Our kids have hearts. They understand when they're being made fun of," Sandy said. "And they can do so much. It may look different, but they can still do it. . . . They have so much to give to society, and they just need to be given a chance. Because they are precious. They are. They all can be functional members of society, given that opportunity. Most of them want that. They want what everybody else is doing. . . . So don't be afraid to befriend them and show them love. Because they're really no different than you and I. We all have a disability in us somewhere."

God's Plan at Work

Sandy has learned that running Barnabas Prep is all about faith and obedience.

"We are going to be obedient to what the Lord has called us to do. We are taking care of the least of these, and we are showing them love. We're loving on the families. This program is as much for the families as it is for the Students, because this is giving [the Students] a safe place to be and their families don't have to worry about them."

Sandy's own faith has grown greatly through being Justin's mom and through her interactions with Prep Students.

"Justin, he's taught me to stop and listen. There's times that I'll say [to him], 'Well, how did you know that? How do you know not to be afraid?' 'Well, God told me,'" she said. "I believe that [our Students] are still enough that they can hear God's small whispers. I watch them in church, and they worship with aban-

Enjoying the Barnabas Prep campus

don. They give it all they've got. They're not pleasing man. They're pleasing the Lord. There are days that I have to step back and think, 'This is childlike faith.' And there are days that I don't have that. They all teach me that."

When Sandy was younger, she used to say her favorite verse was Jeremiah 29:11: "'For I know the plans I have for you,' declares the Lord, 'plans to prosper you and not to harm you, plans to give you hope and a future.'"

Because of the struggles Justin went through, as well as a childhood illness that her daughter faced, there have been times when Sandy questioned the goodness of God's plan. But she has learned to look at life like a tapestry—humans can only see the underside, which is filled with knots, but God looks down from above and sees the complete image, beautiful and whole.

That illustration has given her a different perspective on her life and God's plan in it.

"I went from thinking, 'OK, my life verse is Jeremiah 29:11,' to, 'You know what? This is an Esther story—I was created 'for such a time as this.' Because if I [hadn't] had Justin, and we [hadn't] trusted to send him to Camp at a young age and become invested in the Barnabas family, I wouldn't be where I am today. And, you know, I love being here. I love the Students, the Staff, the families, and it's just—see, I'll cry," she said, tearing up. "Barnabas is that near and dear to my heart, because it made such a difference in our lives."

Today, Sandy can't imagine working anywhere else.

"I can walk into a room, and I would have just seen [the Students] yesterday, and when I go in there, it's like I'm the biggest rock star. They're like, 'Whoo, Sandy!' I tell people, 'Where else can you work that you are a rock star?' . . . I wouldn't trade it for the world."

> "Once I started working with [people with disabilities], I feel like the Lord really taught me a lot about Himself through that experience. I felt like I was finally seeing what it means to love other people [and] to be joyous despite circumstances, because a lot of the people I was working with who were going to Camp were in a lot harder circumstances than I was in, but they were a lot more joyful than I ever was."
>
> – Zach C., Summer Staff and Prep Fellow

CHAPTER 20

A Change of Heart:
Nathan Doss, Barnabas Prep Resident Coordinator

Nathan Doss was sitting in a Christian ministries college class in the spring of 2018 when his professor stormed in and began reprimanding the class for their failure to put what they were learning about ministry into practice.

"He comes in for five minutes and chews us out," Nathan said. "Then he leaves. It's a two-hour class, and we're like, 'Oh, shoot.' We're waiting. We waited twenty minutes to see if he'd come back. He never did."

The experience convicted Nathan deeply, especially in relation to his interactions with people with disabilities. Nathan's mom was a special education (SpEd) teacher, so Nathan had grown up around people with disabilities, yet he had never engaged with them personally.

"I was little, and I never really got the chance to get to know them," he said. "I was just like, 'They're different.' That's all I knew. My mom would always bring them around, and I was just like, 'Mom, why? Why are you bringing them to my birthday party? This is my birthday party.'"

In 2015, Nathan started attending College of the Ozarks just outside of Branson, Missouri, where he studied recreational administration and Christian ministries. Shortly before the dramatic scolding from his professor, one of his friends told him about Camp Barnabas and encouraged him to apply. At the time, Nathan had little interest in working at Camp, but after the experience with his professor, his heart changed.

"I think the Holy Spirit just laid on my heart and was like, 'You need to apply for Camp Barnabas. It'd be challenging and get you out of your comfort zone,'" Nathan explained. "So right after that class, I went and applied for Camp Barnabas, and the rest was history."

Nathan was accepted onto Summer Staff for the summer of 2018.

"It literally changed my life," he said. "I remember leaving, and I was like, 'Man, I want more of this.'"

Nathan loved getting to know Campers, but because each Camp session only lasted a week, he wasn't able to go as deep as he wanted. That fall he made the decision to withdraw from college, and he started substitute teaching, picking up as many SpEd classes as possible.

In November 2018, Nathan was traveling to Branson for a family vacation when a Staff Member from Barnabas Prep called him. "Your name was thrown around for the position of resident coordinator. We'd love for you to interview."

Not super familiar with Barnabas Prep, Nathan asked, "Where are you guys located?"

"Branson."

"I'm actually on my way to Branson right now," Nathan said. "Can we meet tomorrow?"

Before he knew it, Nathan had been hired and was on his way back to Branson. For the past three years, he has worked at Barnabas Prep as a resident coordinator, helping hire and mentor Fellows, lead classes, and plan Student activities. In that time, he met and married his wife and built relationships with many Prep students—two of whom were groomsmen in his wedding.

"Talk about actually getting to know people. I was like, holy cow," Nathan said. "I think that's the best part. . . . I would have never thought two of [the Students] would be groomsmen in my wedding. So yeah, [Barnabas] definitely has changed my life in crazy ways."

Fun and Friendship

Life at Barnabas Prep provides plenty of opportunities for creativity and fun. As part of his job, Nathan leads weekend and evening activities for the Students. Recent activities have included live-action *Angry Birds* complete with giant slingshots, *Minute to Win It* and *Fear Factor* games, an outing to see *Frozen JR.*, trivia nights, trips to Silver Dollar City, and movies outside on a big inflatable TV.

"That's super fun, getting to plan clubs and all the activities Students do on weekends."

Nathan said working at Barnabas Prep has helped him grow in many ways.

"When you work at Prep, you fill so many roles. You're like a parent, you're a friend, you're a brother or sister," he said. "Barnabas Prep has made me a better son. I've called my mom, been like, 'Mom, I'm so sorry for not making my bed or doing the dishes right.' . . . It's made me a better sibling, it's made me a better friend, and honestly a better husband too."

The two Students who were groomsmen in his wedding continue to be good friends today.

"Adam is super quiet. He doesn't say very much, and I'm very talkative. So he taught me . . . man, it's OK to sit and say nothing and just be present and be OK with not doing anything and being relaxed and going with the flow," Nathan said. "Ryan, he's a little bit older, but he has so much wisdom. He's lived so much life, and just getting to hear his stories was so amazing. He taught me so much about patience and how to be a better leader."

A lesson from one of the Prep parents has stuck with him too.

"One of the dads was picking up one of the Students . . . and was pretty upset with me because his Student didn't shave and didn't really look that great and stuff. He talked to me and gave me the reasons why. He's like, 'Hey, as parents, we want the best for our Students. We want our Students to look just great out in public, because people perceive them differently,'" Nathan remembered. "He made me really realize like, man, there's some people who see people with disabilities way differently and think of them as less than. So after he talked to me, I was like, 'Oh, man, he's totally right. I need to kind of have higher standards for myself and hold them to higher standards.'"

That lesson was still ingrained in his mind one summer when he drove his friend Adam to Camp Barnabas and dropped him off for the week. A few days in, he saw a picture of an unshaven Adam online. Immediately, he called up a Staff Member he knew.

"I was like, 'Matthew, Adam needs to shave.' I hung up, and I was like—'Oh, my gosh, I'm like a parent now. Holy cow.' Like he's at Camp, having fun . . . I never thought I'd be doing that." He laughed.

Go With the Flow and Stay in the Word

In some ways, working at Camp Barnabas or Barnabas Prep provides a small glimpse of what Nathan thinks heaven will look like. He remembered someone once describing Barnabas as similar to the four Pevensie children discovering Narnia for the first time—full of wonder and amazement. But at the same time, working at Prep is often challenging and has stretched Nathan in ways he never expected.

One way he's had to change is in terms of flexibility.

"My mom was very structured, and we would show up like twenty to thirty minutes early to things. I was kind of expecting Prep to be super organized and stuff, which we are, but working with people with disabilities, your first plan's never going to work," Nathan explained. "We're doing either Plan B or maybe Plan Z, you know? So it's definitely made me more flexible. I think that was really surprising to me, just how kind of go-with-the-flow you really have to be."

He has also learned that Barnabas Prep is often ground zero for spiritual warfare.

"I've never felt so much spiritual warfare until I've worked at Camp or at Prep," he said. "If I'm not in the Word, I can definitely feel like my day's getting worse and worse."

Intentionally making time to pray and study Scripture has become essential for Nathan. He has learned that, without time with God, he's never as prepared as he needs to be for the questions or problems that Students and Fellows bring to him.

"It's just super important to be in the Word here, because it'll catch up to you if you're not."

The many ways his life has been changed since getting involved with Barnabas continue to surprise him.

"[I] definitely never thought one of my best friends would have Down syndrome," he said. "The lifelong friendships are so amazing."

"[Camp Barnabas] has showed me more of what it means to serve sacrificially and serve as Christ served, looking to others' needs before ours, putting others before ourselves. . . . It has changed my perspective on the world and others, but it has also taught me that people with special needs are awesome. I have absolutely loved that."

– Hannah S., Missionary

CHAPTER 21

A Foundation of Love:
Millie Moyer, Barnabas Prep Resident Coordinator

In early 2020, Millie Moyer was looking for something new. She was living in Branson at the time and knew she wanted to stay in the area. She also knew she wanted to stay in ministry. One opportunity looked promising for a while, but then the door shut, and no other doors seemed to be opening.

Around that time, Millie crossed paths with someone who worked at Barnabas Prep. Millie and the woman recognized each other but couldn't place how they'd met. (Later, they would realize they had mutual friends.) As they talked, Millie shared her heart and explained the kind of opportunity she was hoping and praying to find.

"She just looks at me, and she goes, 'Millie, I have the job for you. I've been praying for someone to come to Barnabas Prep with the same characteristics and the same heart as what you're sharing with me—you're who I need.'"

Millie laughed, remembering her own stunned silence. "I didn't say anything [at first].... I thought, 'Wow, OK.'"

Millie didn't have much prior experience with people with disabilities, but one memory from her freshman year of college came to mind.

"I was in church one morning, and we were worshiping. I looked up, and I noticed that there was this guy who had Down syndrome, and he was just praising the Lord, just unashamed and on fire for the Lord. He was not concerned about what other people thought of him, was not concerned about how he looked—he was just worshiping the Lord," she said.

"That was just such a pivotal moment for me, because at that time . . . I was the one who thought, 'What are people gonna think of me if I raise my hand?' I remember that really struck me, and I actually started kind of tearing up during worship, thinking, 'Wow, God, I want to be that on fire for You and unashamed like he is.'"

As Millie prayed about the Barnabas Prep job her friend had told her about, applying felt right. She was accepted and started at Prep as a resident coordinator in the fall of 2020.

"I was a little nervous coming into it, but more excited than anything. I was eager to learn more, because I hadn't had [much] experience [in this area], but I was confident at the same time, just because I knew that God had wired me with a compassionate heart, with a patient heart, just naturally."

Empowering Students

One of Millie's favorite things about the Students at Barnabas Prep is their willingness to be fully themselves instead of pretending to be someone they're not.

"They are 100 percent unique. There's not another Rachel, there's not another Evan . . . and I love that," she said. "I think we have a tendency—I know I do—to kind of try to just fit in or be accepted or whatever, but they're not seeking that. They're just seeking to be themselves."

She has learned that loving the Students doesn't mean letting them do whatever they want. Like anyone else, the Students need—and deserve—to be challenged to grow as individuals

"They're a lot more capable than some may realize. A lot more capable. Which means accountability is love to them too. . . . Doing things for them is not always loving them, but being patient with them, that's a different thing. Being patient enough with them to teach them and to hold them accountable and to coach them—that's love, not just doing it for them."

At Prep, Students are always encouraged toward greater levels of independence. Millie loves watching Students' confidence in their abilities continue to grow.

"Some of them come in not being challenged, so they don't have confidence in themselves, and they just rely or depend on other people," she said. "Watching them be pushed and then actually be able to do something that they haven't done on their own before and then build their confidence in that so they think, 'Wow, I actually can do that,' or 'Wow, I never thought I could do this on my own.' There have been just sweet little stories of that throughout my time here, which I love getting to see and be a part of."

Investing in Fellows

Millie's role as one of the resident coordinators changes from day to day, though mentoring the Fellows and equipping them to lead and guide the Students is a constant.

"We have about thirteen Fellows right now, and I oversee the women, so I help and assist them as needed," she said. "I'm responsible for recruiting [female] Fellows each year . . . and for investing in them spiritually through biweekly Bible studies. I also facilitate guest speakers to come in to talk through a variety of topics with all the Fellows, such as personality and career assessment tests, résumé building, financial stewardship, health and wellness, Bible overview, discipleship, spiritual disciplines, and more."

Each topic covered in the program aims to help prepare Fellows for their next steps after their nine-month commitment to Prep ends. Millie loves this aspect of her job—getting to pour into the Fellows, who are constantly pouring into the Students.

"For [the Fellows] to have time with the Lord and for them to be poured into and given advice and wisdom and encouragement . . . is huge," she said. "Overall, the Fellow Program is an opportunity to die to yourself, serve others, build life-long relationships, and most importantly grow in your understanding of God's character and personal relationship with Him."

Eyes Fixed on Christ

Millie appreciates getting to be behind the scenes at Barnabas Prep and to help remind people of Prep's "why."

"I just love getting to be a part of the why, and reminding people of why we do what we do," she said. "I think God's reminded me a lot that it's not about me; it's not about us. It's about Him and His glory. We get to serve Him by serving the Students."

Keeping the focus on God makes all the difference in the world.
"Some days, we don't always make the best decisions, we don't always do the right thing. However, with God at the center and with our eyes fixed on Him and seeking what He desires and what would glorify Him, it literally changes everything," Millie said. "The way the Students are treated, the way that Staff are treated, the way that we work together as a team . . . this really is a place where it's outward-focused. It's not about us, so I just can't imagine people doing it if their heart or desire wasn't to serve others . . . [because] it's *hard*. . . . It's so good and so fruitful, but also very hard. But dying to yourself is where life's found."

In the end, it all comes back to relationship—with God and with others.

"Life-on-life discipleship is just on the go. Discipleship doesn't always look like sitting down with someone having coffee and talking about the Bible, but it looks like truly loving them and having fun with them and having a conversation about God on the go. We're building relationships as we're folding laundry. If we're not loving [others], there is no base. There is no foundation. So I think love is the base; [it's] the foundation of everything."

> "I always tell people that Camp Barnabas is the closest thing you'll ever experience to heaven here on earth. It is the most joyful place I've ever been and just feels like home. Even in the midst of sometimes constant chaos,
> my spirit is always at rest when I'm there."
>
> – Madi B., Missionary

CHAPTER 22

A Little Piece of Heaven:
Ashia Puckett, Missionary and Barnabas Prep Fellow

For Ashia Puckett, becoming a Barnabas Prep Fellow has been an opportunity to do missions work right here in the United States.

"I came to Camp Barnabas for the first time in 2018 as a Missionary and did the same in 2019. Growing up, I knew that I wanted to do some sort of mission work, and after going to Camp I realized that I could do mission work in the U.S., not just overseas. It was 2021 when I went on Staff for the first time. That summer was absolutely life changing."

Ashia worked at Camp Barnabas that summer as part of their Extreme Team, a group that heads up activities such as the ropes course, camping excursions, and lifeguarding at the pool. She spent the summer running the ropes course and loved every minute of it.

Partway through the summer of 2021, Nathan Doss and Millie Moyer, the coordinators of Barnabas Prep's Fellow Program,[1] came and spoke to the Summer Staff about Prep.

"It was at that moment I was like, 'Oh, my goodness, this is amazing. God has blessed me with more of an opportunity to do His work, more than just the summer.' So I applied, and I got accepted. I dropped out of college, and now I'm here." Ashia smiled. "It was totally the Lord. I'm very grateful that He allowed the opportunity to happen."

A Fearless Attitude

Both Camp and Prep have influenced Ashia in significant ways. One of the biggest surprises to her when she first started working at Camp was the overwhelming joy of the Campers.

"I get kind of emotional talking about it. But it's just so sweet, watching everyone in this place. Camp is a place where people can come and just be themselves and not be judged. Camp is a place where life-long friendships are made. It's a place that once you come, you just can't get enough."

---

[1] Nathan's story can be read in Chapter 20, and Millie's story can be read in Chapter 21.

Running the ropes course at Camp has given Ashia a front row seat to Campers' courage as well. Over and over, she has seen a Camper overcome some initial nerves or fear to conquer the ropes course and zipline, with the help of a little encouragement from Missionaries and Staff.

One Camper's attitude toward the ropes course particularly impacted Ashia. This Camper was visually impaired and very petite, barely big enough for the smallest harness Ashia's team had, but she approached the ropes course with impressive confidence.

"[Here's] this little girl who is mostly blind, who can conquer the ropes course without absolutely any fear—that's insane to me. I have grown friends who are terrified to go up the ropes course. I am sure that at the beginning, I was also scared—it's something that you have to work up to. However, it just blew my mind how fearless she was," Ashia said. "You know that she trusts that the rope and the person holding the rope is going to keep her safe, and that is such a great representation of how much we are supposed to trust the Lord. Camp has given me such a different outlook on life."

That type of courage, shown by so many Campers, is inspiring to Ashia.

"It's just so encouraging to me for whatever I'm going through. Whether hard things in my life or different trials, I know I can do this. I can keep pushing through, because the Lord is sovereign, and He's created me . . . to go and share His Word, and I can't have worries and trials hold me back. They are supposed to make me trust the Lord and to force me to lean on Him during those times."

Living Unashamed

At Barnabas Prep, Ashia has found herself continually encouraged by the genuine and sincere faith Students display.

"We have this one Student in our house, and she's so sweet and loves the Lord so much. Any time she's doing something that is either scary to her or something that might be uncomfortable, she prays out loud to herself," Ashia said. "That just melts my heart every time, because . . . I see she just has this close relationship with the Lord."

She also loves how the Prep Students are unafraid to be themselves.

"We go to church on Sunday, and they're just jumping up and down praising the Lord. They don't care that everyone else is standing there and watching them—they are jumping up and down. They're spinning around, they're dancing, they're doing all the things. That's so cool, because that's how it's going be in heaven—that's how we all should be worshiping on Sundays and praising our Father."

Being fully oneself and not worrying about others' opinions is an area Ashia hopes to continue growing in personally.

"Being at Prep has helped me realize that the world does not revolve around me. It has helped me see that it doesn't matter what people think of you. Prep is a place where we can grow in our imperfections. And it's just cool, because the

Students are not only growing in who they are, but they are also helping us grow as well," she explained. "The Lord has made us unique and different. I know that through our imperfections Christ gets all the glory. We are made stronger though Him."

Growth in the Lord

The exhaustion brought on by a Fellow's role is very real. Being with the Students twenty-four seven and maintaining the patience that is sometimes required to explain the same thing multiple times can be draining physically, mentally,
and emotionally.

"I think what I've learned through that is [to find] my rest in the Lord whenever I can't find my physical rest, and I don't have time to get that," Ashia said. "My season with Barnabas in general has really given me the opportunity to depend on the Lord more than I ever have. Without Him I could not do this job."

Through seeking to teach and love the Students, Ashia has seen her own understanding of the Lord's love grow.

"They teach me how to love better. I've been able to see how the Lord loves us, even when we aren't listening, even when we're trying to take control of our own situations. I am thankful for that opportunity. The Lord loves us and forgives us without thinking twice about it, and I know that I should do the same."

Keeping the focus on God is an absolute requirement to do the job of a Fellow.

"This is a place where we have to depend on Him every single day. Without Him, I don't think we would be able to love as much as we can, and we wouldn't have the patience. Obviously, we still struggle with that, but it would be completely different if Christ wasn't a part of the picture."

Perhaps because of that deep need, seeking the Lord and His guidance through prayer has become a way of life for Barnabas Prep Staff—one that is evident even to outsiders.

"You can just feel the presence of the Lord in this place," Ashia said. "We've had people who don't come here very often walk into this building and say, 'Wow, I really feel the presence of the Lord in this place'—just because this place is prayed over so much, and there's so much Scripture and so much love poured into this place."

For her part, Ashia is grateful for the chance to be part of Barnabas's work.

"Barnabas is like a little piece of heaven. It's just, it's incredible—Camp and Prep. The work that people do there is just so, so incredible."

> *"Camp has made me into a better person than I was before. It has made me realize that the joy, love, and compassion that I give and receive at Camp can continue into reality. This amazing place has also made me realize how lucky I am to live the life I have."*
>
> *– Kennadi H., Missionary*

CHAPTER 23

Giving It All to God:
Jack Sadler, Barnabas Prep Fellow

Jack Sadler was fighting fires in Colorado when he decided to return to Camp Barnabas for one more summer. A Missionary from 2011-2016 and a Summer Staff Member from 2017-2021, Jack was no stranger to the inner workings of Camp. When he became a firefighter in 2022, fighting both wildfires and structure fires, Jack thought his time at Camp was over, but a transition between departments left him with a couple months off in the summer.

While Jack was working at Camp in 2022, Nathan Doss, one of the resident coordinators for Barnabas Prep,[1] asked him to consider applying for the Fellow Program. Jack and Nathan were on Summer Staff together in 2018, and Jack had learned about Prep when Nathan started working there in 2019. At the time, Jack thought the program sounded interesting but wasn't for him.

"Then Nathan talked to me about it. He's like, 'Hey, we have this position with the Intern Program—I think you'd do well, and I'd love to see you there,' and I'm like, 'Oh no.'" Jack laughed. "But then the Lord told me that was [what] He wanted me to do. So I decided to press pause on my career in the fire service for the time being, and here I am."

Since the fall of 2022, Jack has been working as a Fellow over the Barnabas Prep Interns—Students who have progressed in their studies to the point of being able to live on their own in Intern houses on Prep's campus. Jack's responsibilities include teaming up with another Fellow, Bekah Walker,[2] to teach classes for the Interns and to lead Anchor Co., a business through which Interns make and sell T-shirts and candles.

One of Jack's favorite aspects of Anchor Co. is that it gives Interns real-life work experience that he hopes will help them land other jobs as well.

"We've applied for a lot of jobs with [the Students]. We've brought them in and had the interview or had them apply. So far, a lot of people have said, 'No,

---

[1] Nathan's story can be read in Chapter 20.

[2] Bekah's story can be read in Chapter 24.

Jack at Camper arrival

we're not hiring' . . . [or] 'Yeah, we just don't think they can handle the job.' I think having [Anchor Co.] on their résumé [showing that they] made candles and made shirts and were paid for it . . . [will] prove to other people that, yeah, they have a disability, but they can still do it."

A Wealth of Perspectives

Jack has enjoyed getting to know the Prep Students and has learned that, just like anyone else, they have things they struggle with and things they excel at. For example, Andrew is great at math and friendly conversations, but he sometimes has difficulty with stressful situations. Evan has the best memory of anyone Jack has ever met. He can remember all his friends' birthdays and can figure out the day of the week a person was born based on the date, but sometimes he'll bring up tough topics because he wants to see how a person will react.

"And you don't have to act like that's OK," Jack said. "We'll just simply say, 'Evan, you know better. . . . Do you think that's OK?' He goes, 'No, that's mean. I shouldn't do that.' They are people. They're people that have skills and struggles just like everyone else. You don't have to treat them differently, like they can't make mistakes, or on the flip side, like they can't bring a lot of good things to the table. Just like everyone else, this is a person who is capable of personal growth, and having their feelings hurt, and being a good friend."

Jack has come to value the perspective that each Prep Student has to offer.

"Everything in life is about perspective. Everything is different according to each and every person," he explained. "What might be something huge for me doesn't even matter to someone else. And, of course, things that I don't even think about might be super pertinent for another person. So for instance, there are a couple students here who love Slinkys. Aiden and Jordan love them—Jordan has a giant bag dedicated specifically to Slinkys, and he will lay them all out on his bed and play with them. Aiden has a few too. He will carry one around on his arm every day, and then he'll kind of jiggle it in his hand, so the top few coils jump around on top.

"Prior to coming to Prep, I didn't really care about Slinkys. I think I had one as a kid, but I didn't play with it much. But since being here and getting so close with the boys, they have reintroduced me to Slinkys, and wow, are those things cool! [That's just] one of many things that I have gained an appreciation for since being here with such a diverse group of people to do life with."

Learning to respect each person's perspective and the things they enjoy has been a striking illustration of how God might look at the world.

"You can look at something for hours and think that you totally understand it. And then someone else comes in, and they have this other viewpoint on it. Like, 'Oh, I like this too.' 'Oh, I didn't even notice that. I was so focused on this other aspect, because that's what I've been training my brain to look at.'

"Every single person was made by the Lord, so differently and so specifically that each person has their own incredible perspective, that being here [at Prep], we get to see and get to be part of. . . . It's kind of fun to think of what [God's] perspective must be—each person is just a little piece of the Lord's image. My perspective plus your perspective, your perspective plus Joy's perspective, plus Aiden's perspective—God has all that too."

Letting God Work Things Out

Working with Prep Students has helped Jack see the smallness of many of his own problems, and he has come to admire how infrequently Students worry about their disabilities.

"It's like, 'This is how I should be living. Why am I giving so much weight to this thing that's a problem in my own life?'" he said. "Most of these guys have lived with this their whole lives . . . and they're like, 'It's just the hand I was dealt, and I'm gonna go through life the only way I know how and love the Lord with everything that I have.'"

On the other hand, the Students' occasional stubborn moods have helped Jack gain a new view on how the Lord must sometimes feel toward him.

"You're like, 'What are you doing? Why are you doing this again? We just talked about this.' It kind of makes you realize, oh, wow, I do that all the time with God. Or [I] fall into this sin, and then the Lord calls me back to Himself and talks to me. He's like, 'You know what, Jack, you need to work on this.' 'You're right, you're right.' Next week, same thing."

But Jack has also learned to give himself grace and to trust God to work through his weaknesses. Early on in his experience at Prep, an attempt to drive the Interns into Branson for an activity turned into an illustration of letting go of perfectionism and trusting the process.

"I must have made six wrong turns in a row, because we got lost for so long. [All the Students] in the back were freaking out. I'm sure they're thinking... 'Who's this Jack guy and Bekah girl that we're supposed to trust, and who's driving this van?' We kind of just kept saying, 'Guys, it's OK. We're gonna get there—it's not going to be pretty, but let's just have a good attitude and give ourselves to it.'" He laughed. "I still make wrong turns all the time. . . . [One of the Prep Students] always says, 'Nobody's perfect—God is.'"

That truth brings relief and freedom from striving.

"It's gonna be OK. We'll work it out. Nothing is beyond what the Lord can do. It's hard work here, and sometimes you're gonna have an interaction with someone who just pushes you over the edge, and you can't do it. There's nothing that we can do here without putting our faith in the Lord, but the good thing is, you don't have to. He's got you, He's there, and He's willing to walk with you and carry you in the stretches that you can't really walk anymore, just as long as you give your all to Him and trust Him."

Offering Your Best

Throughout the ten-plus years Jack has been involved with Barnabas, he's learned that, like him, everyone in the organization is simply doing their best and relying on God to make the most of their obedience.

"When I started out at Camp, I was a Barnstormer, and to me, the one-on-one Counselors were just the coolest, they had it all together," he explained. "But then I became a Counselor and realized it's just the same—but those Staffers, you know, they've got it all together! So on and so on up the line, until you realize nobody has got all the answers. I've been in leadership positions at Camp totally making it up as I go along and I'm just praying that it'll all work out.

"It's the same at Prep. You look at the Fellows, and oh, they know what's going on. They've got it all together. The Fellows are looking at Nathan and Millie [the resident coordinators] the same way, Nathan and Millie[3] are looking at Sandy [Prep's director],[4] and we all look at John [the CEO],[5] the same way—which I sometimes still kind of think that John and Sandy have got it all together. But I had a conversation with John a little while ago, and . . . he told me, 'You could wake up tomorrow and die, and your earthly life is over. You thank the Lord for the gift of today, and then do the best you can to be obedient.'"

The bottom line, Jack said, is that no one really knows what they're doing.

"We're just relying on the Lord and kind of saying, 'I don't know what you're gonna do with this, but here's all the bread and fish that I have. You can do something cool with it.' No one's pretending to know what they're doing. I just think the further up you get, the more you realize, 'Oh, no one's got it—except for the Lord.'"

---

[3] Nathan's story can be read in Chapter 20, and Millie's can be read in Chapter 21.

[4] Sandy's story can be read in Chapter 19.

[5] John's story can be read in Chapter 26.

Jack has found that all these experiences he's had at Camp Barnabas and at Barnabas Prep are a little hard to explain to his friends and family back home.

"You know, you get back from the summer, and you're like, 'Dude . . . I worked at Camp this summer, and it was crazy.' And someone else is like, 'Dude, me too.' And you're like, 'No, no.'" He shook his head. "Part of that is just the people who make up Barnabas. The Staff . . . the Students, the Campers—they're just some of the most incredible people you'll ever meet . . . just the way the Lord shines through people and the work being done, is something that isn't talked about enough."

In the end, Jack said, the best way to understand Barnabas is to experience it for yourself.

"[There's] something special about Barnabas that just is really hard to experience if you're not part of it. I think everyone should experience Camp or Prep at some point in their life."

"At home I've struggled with putting my identity in the things I can do to serve others, depending on my own strength, and feeling like I am not doing enough, but after church on Sunday and conversations with a Camper about the verse 'My strength is made perfect in your weakness,' I didn't struggle with that very much at all during Camp."

– Katy S., Missionary

CHAPTER 24

Positioned for a Purpose:
Bekah Walker, Barnabas Prep Fellow

Bekah Walker's path to Barnabas Prep feels almost like a series of accidents, but as she looks back, she can see God's hand at work.

She had never heard of Camp Barnabas or Barnabas Prep until one of her friends was hired for the Extreme Team at Camp in 2021 and encouraged Bekah to think about coming to Camp as a medical intern.

"Through a lot of craziness, I applied and ended up at Camp. I mean, it was crazy. Definitely a God thing that I ended up there," she said.

Through that experience, Bekah heard about Prep's Fellow Program, but she wasn't interested initially. At the time, finishing her undergrad degree in biology took all the time and attention she had.

"Then this summer [in 2022] after I graduated, [I] went to Camp again, on accident almost. I was supposed to be there one week, but I ended up staying for seven weeks."

Bekah spent the summer working in the Well House as a medical intern, and partway through, she impulsively applied to nursing school. When she was accepted, she thought she would spend the next several months attending in-person classes to complete the prerequisites for her program. But two days before the application for Prep's Fellow Program was due, Bekah learned that her courses could be completed online.

Upon hearing the news, Bernadette Losh, Camp Barnabas's executive director of health services,[1] told Bekah, "You have to go to Prep."

"I came and toured [Prep], and I said, 'No, I don't want to do this.' And then God was like, 'No, you have to.'" She laughed. "So now I'm here doing it, and I love it. It's definitely pretty obvious that He put me here on purpose."

Grace through Chaos, Mistakes, and Differences

Even though Prep is where Bekah knows she's supposed to be, the Fellow Program has been a stretching experience.

---

[1] Bernadette's story can be read in Chapter 29.

Along with Jack Sadler, another of the Fellows,[2] Bekah oversees the Students who have progressed far enough in Prep's program to become Interns. This role has included figuring out how to run Anchor Co., a business that sells T-shirts and candles made by the Interns.

In 2021-2022, the Interns learned how to make T-shirts and successfully created two types of candles, but in the 2022-2023 school year, Jack and Bekah worked to turn Anchor Co. into a functioning business that will give the students real-life work experience to help boost their résumés.

"I had no idea what I was coming into working here, so everything has kind of been chaotic and surprising," Bekah said. "I'm someone who likes order, and this is very unorganized, because we are still building the program. But [I'm] learning that's OK and being happily surprised that the chaos is really good."

As a Fellow, Bekah is positioned as one of the Students' teachers, but she has found that she learns just as much from them as they might from her.

"This is really my first time ever doing anything with the disability community. They just have so much potential, and we tend to label them by whatever we think is wrong with them or different about them. There is so much more to them than just that one thing," she said. "Everyone experiences that in some way ... some people are well known for their love of medicine or their whatever, but there's so much more to them than that. The same is true for [our Students]."

One of the biggest lessons Bekah has learned came from an Intern named Joy.

"Sometimes when you get on her for being stubborn or for overreacting to something, she will continue to beat herself up about it. But then give her like ten or twenty minutes—she might bring it up again, but she's basically moved on. She'll be like, 'OK, we're gonna do better next time,'" Bekah said. "I'm someone who holds onto stuff and beats herself up about everything all the time. So learning from her, like, 'No, you're gonna mess up. Only God's perfect, not us,' is a good reminder every day that we're gonna mess up, and it doesn't matter that much. It'll be OK."

It's an attitude that Bekah has begun to appreciate in many other Barnabas Prep Staff as well. In some places she has worked in the past, mistakes have been detrimental, but at Prep, they are only obstacles to be worked through.

"Because [Prep is] a company where almost everyone who participates or works for them is a believer, all of us have the same perspective and mindset, which helps us work together better," she said. "When [a miscommunication or disagreement happens], we still struggle with it because we're human, but all of us still have that mindset of like, 'OK, no, but we're all not perfect—we're all saved by grace.' People are much more likely to forgive and move on and work together to figure things out than in other companies I've worked with."

---

[2] Jack's story can be read in Chapter 23.

Bekah has also found that Barnabas Prep is a continual reminder of how God works through very different people and can use one person's strength to complement another's weakness.

"Jack and I are very different. Millie and Nathan [the resident coordinators][3] are very different. A lot of the people who work together constantly are very different. But it's so obvious that that's for a reason," she said. "Because when I can't handle something, [Jack] can. Or when both of us can't handle it, one of the Students does. There's always someone [in place] that God is using to do whatever His will is, and it's just mind blowing."

---

[3] Millie's story can be read in Chapter 21, and Nathan's can be read in Chapter 20.

> "[Camp Barnabas] is a place where all of God's children are welcome and loved."
>
> – Marsha R., Cabin Parent

CHAPTER 25

In Their Own Words:
Barnabas Prep Students

Barnabas Prep has impacted many: the Staff, the Fellows, the families, and, perhaps most of all, the Students themselves. In this chapter, Students share their experiences at Barnabas Prep and why it means so much to them.

How did you find out about Barnabas Prep?
Sophie: The teacher my first year was a good friend with one of my sister's friends.

Mark: My mom just told me about it.

Cooper: So I found out from the director. Her name is Sandy Miller. So it's a college for kids with disabilities . . . and we have to live in a dorm. We come to school every year, like every Monday through Friday. On Tuesday we do Tie Tuesday, and we go do bowling on Tuesdays. And also, I am volunteering in the office with Miss Megan and Mrs. Laura and Nathan and Sandy. They are amazing people at Barnabas Prep. It's lots of fun here.

What made you want to come to Barnabas Prep?
Liam: I just came here to learn to be independent.

Sophie: Just the community down here.

What are some of your favorite things about being at Barnabas Prep?
Mark: Well, I've gotten to do swimming, swimming in the summer. And I got to go to the Christmas parade. Get to go around places for community integration . . . . What we done in February is we went on a cruise. . . . Next year we'll be going to Cozumel.

Cooper: So my favorite is to make some new friends. I like to play basketball. Sometimes I watch some very fun movies. . . . [We] talk about God and Jesus. . . .

Life at Barnabas Prep

He's our very Good Shepherd. . . . Anything here at Barnabas Prep is amazing. And I would say three things. I must thank Sandy for putting me in this program, and I want to thank my mom and my dad for putting me in this program. And I love it here. I'm coming back for my second year.

Sophie: Maybe all the friends I've made. Working. Going on the cruises. . . . We do a cruise every February, and we go to Mexico. And we just go there for like a week. We just hang out on the boat and stuff.

Liam: Well, I just, I came here to be independent. So someday, when I like leave here, I can live on my own. Find a house on my own with four roommates.

Can you tell me about the friends you've made here?
Cooper: Oh, yes. So I made Mark, Liam, David, Parker, Lucy, Charlotte—they all are amazing. I have one friend [here] I knew from high school. His name is Cole.

Sophie: One of my good friends, Paige, she and I are both Chiefs fans.

Liam: My best friend is Evan. He's my best friend here, and my other best friend is Aubrey. She's one of my best friends. We grew up together. . . . We went to high school together.

What are some things you've learned here?
Mark: I've learned about the brother Jesus. I learned that He's the Son of God, and He's the Messiah. I learned how to take out the trash. And do a dishwasher.

Cooper: So I learn about the Bible and PE and health, and we do reading groups. Like, we go to the library. Sometimes and only on Fridays, we go somewhere

where we have a job. Like an internship. It's super fun. On Fridays, we do water aerobics. So water aerobics is a workout in the pool . . . it's very fun.

Sophie: How to do laundry. Maybe how to [do] the hygiene better by myself.

Do you have a favorite class or activity here?
Sophie: It's Bible application. We have a daily devotional, and we go through it every day.

Liam: I like PE. I like it here at PE. We play games, like exercise and do warm-ups, and we do stretches, and we do fun stuff, like we do stations and weight lifting, and we do curls and arm circles.

What do you want to do when you finish at Barnabas Prep?
Mark: Be a cashier at Walmart.

Sophie: I like where I am. I work at the Legends Theater. I shred paper there.

Liam: I want to get a job in a coffee shop. I worked at a coffee shop called Not Your Average Joe. . . . A lot of my friends work there. . . . My job is to make sure all the bathrooms are clean, and make sure the basement is clean, and make sure all the dishes are clean and put away, and make sure the customers get their coffee, and make sure, like, all the tables and floors are looking good and all the customers are doing good. . . . I'm gonna tease them and say like, "Here's your coffee. Oh, if you don't want it, I'll have it. You want it? Are you sure? I'll drink it for you. I'm just kidding. Here you go."

If someone didn't know anything about Barnabas Prep, what would you want to tell them about it?
Mark: I would tell them that Barnabas Prep is a great place. You get to learn about Jesus and God and how to take care of yourself after you graduated.

Sophie: That the Fellows and the Staff are really great, and you meet a lot of good people here.

Cooper: Well, first you have to apply and take a tour by Director Sandy, and she will take a tour. If you want to go to Barnabas Prep, you better ask your mom and dad or your siblings, and you have to go to Barnabas Prep. If you accept for Barnabas Prep, you can be happy. . . . I got in early December from last year. That was a fun time. I was so excited. I jumped, and I was laughing and smiling. It was fun.

Part 4

"Camp Barnabas is a place where walls come down, connections are made, and the gospel is communicated in word and deed. Camp Barnabas means laying your life down for the sake of others and finding out that really is where Jesus is waiting to meet you."

– Garrett B., Cabin Parent

CHAPTER 26

A God-Sized Vision:
John Tillack, CEO

For John Tillack, balancing business acumen and a deep-seated commitment to ministry has been a lifelong journey. While both passions have played important roles, he finds his true calling where the two intersect.

Growing up, John looked up to his father, Dave Tillack, as a role model. When John was twelve, Dave transitioned from a successful business career in Tampa, Florida, to running a nonprofit mission organization in Tulsa, Oklahoma. This shift left a lasting impression on John, shaping his perspective on service and humility.

"My dad always said, 'When you're called to be a servant, don't stoop to be a king,'" John remembered. "That wisdom resonated deeply with me."

During John's college years at Oral Roberts University, he spent his summers working at Kanakuk Kamps. He gave his heart to Christ at a young age and felt his faith grow through his involvement with camp. As his commitment to his faith grew, John also felt drawn toward the business world.

"There was this pull—I loved ministry, and I loved business. I really had an entrepreneurial drive. . . . I saw business as a really fun game, where the goal was to produce a product that hopefully people wanted and it made them happy," he explained. "[And yet] I just felt like camp was this beautiful way to step out of the insanity of the world, turn it off for a minute, and just be still, have fun, hear God, and be filled with hope."

Through his college experiences as a counselor at Kanakuk Kamps, John came to value camp as a place for healing, reflection, and connection with God, and he began to dream of one day running his own camp.

"That was my north star—if I could do anything, you know." He laughed. "I think a lot of people say, 'If I can do anything, I'd sail a boat around the world,' but mine was, 'I want to run a camp.'"

After graduating from college, John's career journey led him on a winding path, from roles in corporate sales and management to a decade at Promise Keepers men's ministry. During those years, he also married his wife, Kamela, and they had four children.

A turning point came in 2002 when John crossed paths with Gregg Bettis, CEO of Kids Across America Kamps (KAA), a camp serving urban youth. Gregg offered John a job as KAA's vice president of marketing and development. The offer changed the course of John's life, leading him to move his family from Denver, Colorado, to Branson, Missouri, where they would spend the next fifteen years.

"It stretched me," he said. "It was great for my family, because they grew up at camp. I was able [to see them] every day in the summer, and they were able to share and grow in mutual love for summer camp ministry. We spent hundreds of hours on ski boats for fifteen summers and ate lots of pizza at the Table Rock Lake Pizza Hut."

His years at KAA were deeply enriching for both him and his family, but after a decade and a half with the ministry, John began to sense God nudging him in a new direction once again.

Joining Barnabas

From his KAA office in Branson, John had a perfect view of the Barnabas Prep campus, which happened to be located across the street in a reconfigured yellow Victorian house. John didn't know much about Barnabas's ministry at the time, but he recalls watching out the window as Students and Fellows tossed a football or square danced in the front yard, always appearing to be having a great time.

At one point, the CEO of Barnabas approached John and asked if he would consider becoming the head of fundraising for the Barnabas Foundation, an umbrella ministry dedicated to managing operations for Camp Barnabas and Barnabas Prep. Content in his position with KAA, John thanked him for the offer but turned it down.

However, not long after, in early 2018, Barnabas's CEO again approached John with a different job offer as the executive director of Barnabas Prep. This time, John was torn.

"I thought, 'No. I'm in my nice little nest. I like my nest—it's safe and predictable.' But I was really conflicted."

Kamela urged John to at least visit Barnabas Prep, hoping the experience would bring him clarity. So he did. By the end of the visit—though changing jobs still felt like a challenge—John felt God leading him. He was reminded of the daily view of joy he saw from his office window and the love and care he saw demonstrated by the Fellows and Students when he toured Prep. It was a true revelation for John.

"I [had] watched these Fellows caring for these adults with disabilities. And I saw these young men and women who had a variety of unique and special needs who just wanted to love, develop relationships, and be in community. All of the things I worried about and was concerned with each day . . . I quickly realized they're not thinking about or worrying about those things. They were just free to love. I just thought, 'Wow, what is this life? Is this what God intended for us when He created this perfect world, that we didn't carry worry or fear or stress?'"

Intrigued by this realization, he said "yes" and accepted the position.

"I felt like God was just saying, 'Let's go have an adventure.' So I jumped, and it was terrifying."

Five months later, however, John's career took another turn. As he was still settling into his new role as executive director, the mantle of CEO of Barnabas was unexpectedly passed to him.

Faced with daunting financial challenges, John embarked on a journey of rebuilding the organization. Every morning before work, he would go into his closet at home and get flat on his face to pray.

"The ministry was broken and upside down in debt," he said. "I realized I couldn't make it work. I just would beg God, 'Lord, if you want this thing to keep going, do a miracle.'"

Over the next several months, John watched as God began working miracles each and every day. Together, John and his team navigated the storm by making tough decisions, restructuring, and even selling assets. Through a combination of collective effort and unforeseen blessings, Barnabas emerged from that season debt-free, something John attributes to the power of unwavering faith.

"It will never be a testament of 'John, this great businessman.' It was John, scared to death, pleading with God. 'God, if this is what you want, show me who I need to talk to,' or 'You're going to have to do it, Lord.' So for the last [five years], we've watched Him rebuild it. . . . It has been a walk of faith, and God has been so evident."

Dreams for the Future

Today, John likens his role of CEO to that of a pilot.

"I tell people I'm flying the plane, turning the dials. I'm making sure we get to our next city safely and that we don't run out of fuel. I have this amazing crew that's keeping the plane running, keeping the passengers happy," he said. "This isn't a 100-person staff—it's a small team of thirty-two people between Prep and Camp, and we'll have five or six thousand people at Camp in the summer. I'm just so proud of them."

John's vision for the future of both Camp and Prep is rooted in providing solace to families who have cared tirelessly for their loved ones with disabilities. While he knows Barnabas can't solve every problem that parents and guardians face, John wants them to know that they're seen and supported.

One memory stands out that illustrates the need for a place like Barnabas. It was opening day for a week at Camp when a beat-up car pulled in, muffler dragging, smoke pouring from its engine, paint completely oxidized. The couple driving the car were in their seventies or eighties. As John watched, a fifty-something-year-old man with Down syndrome jumped out of the back of the car, whipped off his shirt, and started running toward the pool.

"He'd been coming to Camp for twenty years . . . I then watched as six of our counselors chased after him, as he was bound and determined to go swimming. . . . I don't know [the parents'] story, but I know they're poor, and they had cared for their son for his entire life, and he can't wait to go to Camp each year," he said. "I look at all these parents, and they're tired. For most people, you have children, and they graduate from high school or college and go live their lives, and then you, as parents, get to live yours again. But for most Barnabas parents, it's not that way."

John envisions one day building a retreat center for families of people with disabilities—a safe haven where they can find respite and support. Additionally, he hopes to expand housing at Prep so Students can stay with their community longer. He dreams of creating new vocational opportunities—things like building a greenhouse where Students can learn how to grow and sell plants or creating a bed and breakfast with a coffee shop where Students can work.

"It doesn't even scratch the surface [of the challenges people in the disability community face], but in our little world, it might have a little impact."

As John reflects on his many dreams for the future of Camp and Prep, he says he needs to stop thinking and trying to figure everything out and just let God work, just as He has ever since Barnabas's beginning over thirty years ago.

"God just keeps raising people up who say, 'Hey, what is going on at Barnabas?' And then they say, 'I think I'd love to get involved.'" He shrugged. "I don't know—there's just this vision. It's amazing. This place is a gift. It is really hard stuff sometimes, but it's awesome. And it's growing. It's really growing, and it feels like a rocket ship blasting off."

In everything he does, John seeks to attribute Barnabas's successes to a higher calling, and he views each accomplishment as evidence to God's guidance.

"I just always pray for God-sized visions that can't come back to me or [anyone else] and go, 'Oh, it's because we had this idea, and we did it,'" he said. "I want the vision and dreams to be bigger than us. I want my staff and I to say, 'No, this is God's deal. He loves these kids and their parents more than we can ever imagine.'"

John sees Barnabas as an example of the power that faith and love have to transform lives. At the end of the day, Barnabas is God's, and John is grateful to play a role in something so much larger than himself.

> "[Camp Barnabas] means home. I don't feel like I'm at Camp when I'm there; it feels like I am walking around a place that I've known forever."
>
> – Jillian C., Missionary

CHAPTER 27

Walking with the Hurting:
Melissa Pardeck, Parent and Executive Assistant/Development Specialist

Today in 2023, Melissa Pardeck works in Barnabas's development department and provides administrative support to CEO John Tillack. But when she was first introduced to Camp Barnabas in 2012, it wasn't as a prospective employee but as a grieving parent.

Six years before, her then-seven-year-old son, Chase, attended Kanakuk Kamps for a week in June 2006. Less than a month after he came home, out of the blue, he had a seizure.

"That led us to find that he had a brain tumor about the size of a quarter. It was centrally located in his brain," Melissa explained.

Distraught, Melissa and her husband flew Chase to Little Rock, Arkansas, where they were able to get him into Arkansas Children's Hospital. Only a few days later, Chase had surgery to remove as much of the tumor as possible.

"We stayed maybe three more days in the hospital, and then the kid was sent home and was totally normal. You wouldn't even know anything had ever happened except for the scar on his little head."

When the next summer rolled around, Chase begged to go back to Kanakuk. With his doctor's permission, Chase was able to attend camp the next two summers. However, by 2009, the effects of the tumor had become more pronounced again.

"They could never totally remove it—there were just portions that they could get. And then . . . it just metastasized, basically," Melissa said.

In 2012 Chase's doctor delivered the news no parent ever wants to hear: "There's nothing more we can do."

Despite the diagnosis, Chase was still a normal thirteen-year-old boy—and he wanted to return to camp one last time. However, due to his medical needs, Kanakuk was no longer an option.

Melissa had heard about Camp Barnabas through her job at Kids Across America (KAA), Kanakuk's camp for urban youth.

"People would call and say, 'My child's in a wheelchair—can he come to camp?' I'd have to say, 'Sadly, no, we can't accommodate him, but I have heard of another camp in our area,' and I would just give them the phone number for Camp Barnabas. But that was really the extent of my knowledge of it. I'd never been to Camp [Barnabas]. I didn't even know where it was."

They didn't have the money to send Chase to Camp Barnabas at the time, but Chase was able to go through Camp's scholarship program.

"We show up in July of 2012," Melissa said. "Chase is not feeling the greatest, but just being at Camp, that was all that mattered."

After dropping Chase off, Melissa and her husband were able to spend their week focusing on their daughter, then ten years old, who—due to Chase's illness—"was kind of put on the backburner those last six years." They spent the week doing anything their daughter wanted and all had the best time.

Due to the severity of Chase's illness, he was only able to stay one or two nights in his cabin with the other Campers, spending the rest of his time in the Well House. But he still had a fantastic week.

"What stands out to me is his cabin mates would come and spend their time with Chase in [the Well House]," Melissa said. "It just blew me away. They would come and play board games, while he's just lying in bed. They'd just include him in whatever they were doing. I thought that was *so* sweet."

She also loved that Chase got to experience so many activities he loved, like ziplining, thanks to the way Barnabas had adapted things.

"Chase got to do all those things," she said. "Just the things he got to experience that he never thought he would get to experience again is pretty powerful."

When they came to pick Chase up at the end of the week, Melissa remembers crying over the various stories from his time at Camp. As they drove through the gate, she had a strong, inexplicable impression that she would do something with Barnabas someday.

She didn't know what that would look like—if it would mean working there or donating time or money to the ministry.

"But it just blew me away, what I saw and what we experienced as a family. I knew right then that I wanted to be a part of it."

Perfect Timing

Chase's last summer was extra sweet, in part due to his experience at Barnabas. He passed away that fall, on September 4, 2012.

The grieving process was long and hard. Melissa and her husband ended up going through a painful divorce in the aftermath of Chase's illness. Melissa's conviction that she would someday be involved with Barnabas faded into the background for a time.

A few reminders of that summer remained though. One of them was Chase's Missionary, Chloe.

"To this day, we are friends," Melissa said. "We're in each other's lives. I mean, she will always be a part of us. She would send me flowers on Mother's

Day or a card and [was] just the sweetest, sweetest person. So that friendship came out of that week too, with our Chloe—we call her our Chloe."

Another reminder came when John Tillack,[1] who Melissa had worked with for fifteen years at KAA, became CEO of Barnabas in 2018. That same year, Melissa worked as a database manager for Barnabas for a brief stint, but she ultimately returned to KAA. She took a development position—something she had never done before—and worked there for three more years.

In 2021, a position as an executive assistant and development specialist came open at Barnabas, and John Tillack asked Melissa to apply.

"I really want you to pray about this. I think you would be a good fit here," he told her.

Though Melissa had wanted to get involved with Barnabas, the decision to leave KAA after twenty-five years was still difficult. But the timing and the position both seemed right.

"It was a long time coming, but it was God's perfect timing and His perfect plan."

Other than Chase's experience at Camp, Melissa had never spent much time around people with disabilities until she started working at Barnabas. She offices out of Barnabas Prep in Branson and says the Students have taught her so much.

"I'm just more aware of the fact now that they want to be asked about their disability," she said. "That's been really eye-opening for me that, you know, 'Hey, if you have questions about—why is this happening? Or what is your story?' They love to tell their story."

Her experiences at Barnabas have also helped her realize the importance of noticing and reaching out to parents of children with disabilities.

"When I see a mama with a child with a disability, just to be like, 'You're doing a great job today. You're doing amazing. You're a phenomenal person.' And maybe offering help: 'Hey, can I help you with that? Can I carry their plate for you over there?' I think it's made me just be more aware of my surroundings."

Having experienced Camp as a parent gives Melissa an extra dose of empathy for Barnabas parents and a deeper understanding of their need for respite.

"Caring for a child or an adult in your home who has a disability or an illness—you don't ever get a break," she said. "And not that [the parents are] wanting one, but they need one. I think the respite time is just huge and the encouragement that comes along with it. I mean, not only is their son or daughter loved on as soon as they come in the gates, but as a parent, they're loved on too... I think that's huge."

Running to the Lord

Losing a child can easily drive someone away from faith. For Melissa, though, Chase's illness drove her straight into the Lord's arms.

---

[1] John's story can be read in Chapter 26.

"When Chase got diagnosed, my world fell apart. The people who were there to support me and encourage me and lift me up—I don't know how people who don't have faith in the Lord get through situations like what I went through."

Specifically, she says the Lord taught her to let go of her need to be in control.

"I didn't think I was a control freak until things started [falling apart]. Then I'm like, 'Oh, I want to be in charge.'"

Over the past several years, God has helped her learn to let go and trust Him more.

"I just kind of always had a word picture of the tighter I hold on to something, God is just trying to take my fingers off that rope and saying, 'Let go. Let go of the rope. I've got you.' I remember saying to someone one time, 'I'm holding on by a thread.' And they said, 'Then let go of the thread. You can let go.'" She smiled. "That has been my biggest takeaway."

Over time, Melissa's grief and loss have become things the Lord has used in her role at Barnabas as she seeks to listen to and encourage parents who are struggling—something she is uniquely suited to do.

"Especially if their son or daughter has passed away—I just feel really connected to Camper families or donor families, any families [who have experienced] that. I think God uses me in that aspect, just to help walk alongside people when they're grieving and hurting," she said.

"Sadly, Barnabas is full of that. There's just a lot of struggles and parents who are struggling and hurting. I think that's why [the Lord] has me here too, just to try to be an encouragement."

> "I laughed more times than I can count at Camp. I became so close to Jesus in that week and felt His presence like I've never felt before."
>
> – *Ella Doughtery, Missionary*

CHAPTER 28

A Profound Impact:
Don, Jennifer, Makena, and Isabella Hubbs, Parents, Sibling, and Camper

When Don and Jennifer Hubbs reflect on the past decade, they view Camp Barnabas as a deeply meaningful part of their family's journey.

"We are extremely grateful for and blessed by this wonderful organization and the individuals who willingly serve families like ours," Jennifer said.

The Hubbs family first got connected with Camp Barnabas in 2013 when Don and Jennifer began looking for a summer camp for their daughter Isabella, who has autism and mild cerebral palsy. When they discovered Camp Barnabas, they signed both their daughters up for a week: Isabella, or Bella, as a Camper and Makena as a Sibling.

"I'll never forget the first time our girls attended Camp," Jennifer said. "We met families who had traveled great distances to ensure their children could be a part of this experience. We met Missionaries and Staff Members from across the country who were ready to dedicate a week or more to serving our girls and all the other Campers. Tears of joy welled up in our eyes as we realized we had found a special place—a place many refer to as heaven on earth. A place where strangers showered God's love and kindness upon the least of His children."

Initially, Bella had some reservations about attending Camp.

"On the first night, I cried because I missed my mom," she said as she thought back on her first week.

But Makena comforted her, and as the week unfolded, Bella's tears turned into smiles. By the end of the week, she confidently told Jennifer that "it was the best time ever."

Makena, on the other hand, fell in love with Camp Barnabas from the moment she arrived.

"My first experience was running through Camper arrival, and oh my goodness, your heart skips a beat because it's so much fun. Seeing how everyone cheers each other on touched my heart deeply," she said. "Just being there and having people understand that I'm a Sibling of someone with disabilities and connecting with kids like me was truly special. My Counselor was also a Sibling, and I thought, 'I want to be like her when I grow up.'"

For Don and Jennifer, it was easy to see that the week had been a success, and Camp Barnabas soon became a yearly part of their family's routine.

"That's all those kids talked about for the next six months is how much they'd loved it there," Don said. "Bella met a friend who is still a friend today, and her Counselors almost every year have become friends. . . . The same with my daughter Makena—the kids she's met here have become her best friends."

Friendships and Service

Don and Jennifer had hoped both of their daughters would cherish their summer camp experiences and build lasting friendships. It quickly became apparent that both those goals could be accomplished at Camp Barnabas.

"Bella formed many friendships, but none as profound as her bond with another Camper she met a few years ago named Ava," Jennifer said.

"I met my friend [Ava] at Barnabreak," Bella said. "She was in my cabin. . . . I thought she understood me. . . . I was kind of interested about her life mostly, and we became friends."

For Bella, Camp Barnabas became a safe community.

"One thing that surprised me [about Camp] is just how much people are accepting and how loving they are. They just want everyone to be like brothers and sisters here," she said.

Through the Sibling Program, Makena built deep connections with other kids who understood the unique challenges of having a brother or sister with disabilities. After two years of attending Camp as a Sibling, Makena decided she wanted to serve as a Barnstormer.

Jennifer remembers initially trying to dissuade Makena, citing the challenges and responsibilities she already has on a daily basis as a sister to someone with special needs, but Makena's determination prevailed. She volunteered first as a Barnstormer and later as a Missionary.

"Through the years, Makena's journey as a Missionary has given her the chance to be a true blessing, not just to the Campers she's been paired with, but also to their families," Jennifer said.

For Makena, serving has been an opportunity for personal growth.

"I've learned a lot of patience," she said. "I've just learned how to be a better person honestly."

One particularly meaningful experience stands out from when she served as a Missionary and hung out in the pool with a Camper who used a wheelchair. Later that night, the Camper thanked Makena and the other Staff for the experience.

"She said, 'That is the closest I've ever felt to walking before,'" Makena remembered. "And it was like, 'Oh my gosh. I was able to do that for her.' I'm tearing up [thinking] about it, because it's something so little that you don't think about. It's like, 'Oh I'm just taking her to the pool to hang out,' and it was so big for her. She's like, 'I got to walk—I got to feel what it was like to move and stand up on my feet.' It was just an amazing moment to be there and be able to do that."

Makena speaks from experience when she says Camp is a transformative place.

"I think what people need to know is that [Camp Barnabas is] a little slice of heaven, and I think they should also know miracles do happen here. A lot of great things are happening at Camp," she said. "It's one of the best camps around. It's different than just a regular summer camp. . . . It truly will change your heart and make you feel something."

Through their daughters' involvement with Camp, Don and Jennifer have gotten to know a lot of other young people who have served as Missionaries, and they've hosted many of them in their home over the years. Don recalled how often he has talked with teenagers and young adults who have chosen to pursue careers helping people with disabilities because of their experiences at Camp Barnabas.

"When I talk to the young people who are here, I realize just what an impact it has on so many of them," he said. "It's such a cleansing effect for a kid to come down here for a week . . . and work hard . . . [and] help other people and find out there's a different level inside of them they never knew existed."

The Goodness of God

Today, Don serves on the board of the Jedel Family Foundation, an organization founded by Kansas City businessman Harrison Jedel, and he also served on the board of directors for Camp Barnabas for several years. The Jedel Family Foundation has provided funds to help Camp Barnabas build a new cafeteria and an adaptive art center.

"If philanthropy aims to improve the well-being of humankind, I can't think of any organization with a more profound impact than Camp Barnabas," he said.

Don says he is at a point in life where he thinks a lot about legacy. He has learned the importance of having a mission in life that is more than just making money, traveling, or having fun.

"I would tell all executives or business people, when you get ready to sell your business . . . and you want to retire . . . whatever you do, if you don't have a mission in life that you're going to work on, just keep working at whatever you're doing or start finding that other mission in life," he said. "Find something like Camp Barnabas or [a charity] that gets under your skin and then get involved with it. It'll make your life a lot better."

Don and Jennifer have seen Camp Barnabas's impact on many people over the past ten years.

"For us, it is abundantly clear that Camp Barnabas is an instrument through which God transforms hearts, instills the value of serving others above oneself, and nurtures joy and kindness in the lives of countless individuals," Jennifer said.

The Hubbses believe Camp Barnabas is a place that encourages and inspires faith—in God and in people.

"We all question our faith some days, right?" Don said. "But what happens with Barnabas is it just keeps reminding you that God's out there. . . . If you are lacking in faith and you come [to Camp Barnabas] for an hour or a week or a day, it'll reaffirm your faith, not only in God, but in man, in the goodness of people."

Jennifer agrees.

"Even today, our hearts swell with emotion as we approach Camp's entrance, and often, tears flow," she said. "The goodness of God abounds in this place, Camp Barnabas, where people wholeheartedly live out the gospel through acts of kindness and love. We are grateful."

"Camp Barnabas has given me a greater love for the people God loves to uplift: the ones the world sees as 'less than' but God sees as the greatest. Serving them is serving Him."

– Mary H., Cabin Parent

CHAPTER 29

Deep Joy and Heavy Responsibility:
Bernadette Losh, Executive Director of Health Services

The Well House is busy even in the middle of the afternoon. A cool respite from the summer heat, the Well House serves as the Camp clinic, staffed each week of the summer by an average of one or two doctors, ten nurses, four interns, and two Well House assistants. The doctors, nurses, and assistants are usually new each week and have all taken a week's vacation time from their day jobs to volunteer at Camp.

Two volunteer medical professionals sit at the front desk, doing intake and funneling patients through to get the proper care. An overheated Camper comes in and is taken to one of the rooms down the hall to get cooled off. A teenage Missionary has a sprained ankle. Another Camper has a light cough that a Camp doctor checks out to be sure it doesn't indicate something more serious.

Directing the busyness is Bernadette Losh, or Miss B., as many of the doctors and nurses call her. Depending on the time and day of the week, she might be found training her team for the week, coaching an intern through a procedure, talking with one of her favorite Campers, or organizing a tortilla slap for her team—a game in which two people fill their mouths with water and take turns slapping each other with tortillas until one laughs and spits out the water.

"Our stressful times are very stressful. [Our team members] need to talk to each other and have an outlet," Bernadette said. "And also, I want them to come back, you know? So I think it's really important that when we have downtime we're doing a lot of fun stuff, a lot of bonding."

That fun also includes a different theme each day of the week, such as Mustache Monday or Taco Tuesday, complete with fun costumes, and occasionally fun outings like a float trip.

"I don't want anybody to feel uncomfortable, unwelcome, or stressed when they walk into the Well House. I don't want that atmosphere," Bernadette said. "[My team members] don't want to volunteer and take their week of vacation to come and be in a place like that. It's just, it's not going to happen while I'm here. We're gonna have fun."

One Step at a Time

A few years ago, Bernadette wouldn't have imagined herself filling the role she does today. She never went to camp as a child, nor did she send her children to camp. But looking back, she can see how God prepared her for this.

She started her career at Ozarks Community Hospital in 1995 as a labor and delivery nurse, then worked her way up to being a clinic manager. Soon she was managing multiple clinics. Later on, though, she began to feel a tug on her heart to pursue a master's degree in organizational leadership.

"But you know, I have kids, and I'm like, I'm too old for that," Bernadette said.

But she continued to have the sense that this was what she was supposed to do. Finally, she no longer knew why she was waiting, so she started a master's program at Evangel University in Springfield, Missouri, and graduated in 2019.

At the time, Bernadette was managing twenty-five clinics throughout Missouri, Oklahoma, and Arkansas, and the constant travel—plus the demanding, fast-paced culture of her work—left her feeling exhausted and burnt out.

"I didn't realize how much I was starting to resent that culture until I was in my master's program. . . reading about where I wanted to work and the culture that I wanted to work in. That's what kind of pushed me to start thinking about something new."

After two years of looking and still not finding the right opportunity, Bernadette remembers crying as she left work, asking the Lord where He wanted her.

Bernadette with a Camper

Then a friend became Barnabas's director of marketing and communications.

"She texted me and said, 'Hey, we're starting this new position [executive director of health services]. Would you be interested?' She sent me the job description, and I was like, 'That could be exactly what I'm looking for.' I interviewed, and here I am. It's totally opposite of what I was doing, but looking at how I learned how to deal with people and lead a team, all of that just comes into play here."

A Weighty Responsibility

Her first summer at Camp Barnabas, in 2021, was filled with surprises.

"Something happened every single week that changed my perspective of how I'm going to operate in this position and how I view Barnabas."

One of her biggest realizations was that Camp is just as much for the parents and guardians as it is for the Campers.

"I thought this Camp was [only] for the Campers, and it is not," she said. "Campers . . . they come in, they have a great week, and they're so happy. But the parents go as hard as I go or harder fifty-two weeks of the year, and I'm here nine, and that blows my mind."

The realization of just how much Camp parents give hit home in week two when Bernadette thought they might need to send a Camper home for health reasons. The parents, however, were reluctant to come pick up their Camper.

At first, Bernadette was indignant. She complained about the parents' reaction to Craig Swanson, a volunteer physician from California. Craig's response stopped her in her tracks.

"B., they've been waiting for this day for two years, because we canceled Camp in 2020."

That was all it took for Bernadette to realize the depth of parents' need for Camp. From then on, she decided she would do whatever she could to make sure parents had an uninterrupted week of rest.

To do that, Bernadette and her team must care for a vast array of needs. Some weeks have a specific focus. For example, one week serves Campers with intellectual or developmental disabilities, while another serves Campers with physical disabilities. However, other weeks are open to Campers with any kind of disability or illness, which means that within the space of one week, Bernadette's team may offer care to Campers with cerebral palsy, diabetes, Down syndrome, seizures, and any array of other rare illnesses and disabilities that an average person has never heard of.

The weight of responsibility is heavy.

"People's lives are at stake here in a big, big way," she said. "They're fragile. And all the families that bring their Campers here, they're counting on me."

One way Bernadette counteracts that weight is to make sure she spends some time outside the Well House, watching the sheer joy of the Campers as they laugh and interact and dance at the evening Wrap Up parties. She's also learned the necessity of turning her biggest fears over to God and trusting that He's going to take care of the Campers.

"Because otherwise I find myself . . . looking at everyone, walking around, like, 'Who's coughing? What's happening? What have I missed?' That happens to me often, where I have to go and get my Bible and get back in the Word and just let it go, because the 'what-ifs' are too much.

"I've learned a lot of patience, a lot of trusting in the Lord. I don't feel equipped to do this job. Daily, I think about leaving. But just learning to really rely on God to bring me [medical professionals] who can surround me so that we can keep everybody safe has been humbling and a good life lesson."

The Transformative Power of Camp

Bernadette also finds encouragement in all the life-changing experiences happening around her every summer.

"I think it doesn't really matter who you are, you'll come, and you'll be changed [no matter what] you're struggling with. These Campers will teach you a lot—patience, kindness. Just look around and you see so much goodness here. You see fourteen-year-olds serving, singing while they're cleaning a bathroom?" she said with disbelief. "It gives you hope in humanity, truly, because everybody wants to come together to make Camp happen for these families. It's really a big deal, and it really surprises me daily, and I'm like, why am I surprised every day by what God's doing here?"

The past two summers, Bernadette has loved watching her medical interns learn and grow.

She recalled one intern, Gabi, who planned to start physical therapy training in the fall. In Week Four, Gabi took a Camper under her wing, who experienced a lot of pain due to cerebral palsy and used a communication device that tracked with his eyes.

"[Gabi] just spent that week learning how to communicate with him and learning how to help him with his pain. And I just said, 'That's great. You be with him all week.' He had a great week, he ended up going to speak at a college, and she went there to hear him. They'll have this forever bond . . . and I think that really helped kind of [give her] a burst of energy into her PT program."

Another intern, Abbie, refused to listen when Bernadette told her at the beginning of the summer that she would be an incredible nurse.

"She put up her hand to stop me and said, 'I don't know what I'm doing with my life.'"

Bernadette remained quiet on the matter for the rest of the summer, and then on the last day of Camp, Bernadette found Abbie sitting in the med room on her laptop.

"B., I just applied to nursing school," she said.

"Where?"

"In Springfield, but I have nowhere to stay."

Bernadette with Campers

"Well, I guess you're moving in with me," Bernadette said.

So she did. Today, Abbie is in nursing school, getting straight A's.

Bernadette has also seen Camp's impact within her own family. Her nephew, who is autistic, attends as a Camper.

"To see him breaking out of his shell and talking to his Missionary when he comes—it has really helped him be able to interact with people outside of Camp."

Bernadette's daughter, who has Crohn's disease, has been serving as a Missionary for the past couple of years.

"For her to see that there are people who have much bigger burdens than she does . . . yeah, it's difficult, and yeah, she does have pain, and she does have to go to the doctor and all these things and get an injection every two weeks. But to see that everybody has a burden to bear, whether you can see it or you can't see it, I think that has changed her perspective."

Camp has had a significant impact on her husband, Mark, as well. Mark's brother Michael was born with Down syndrome and passed away before Mark and Bernadette met. She had always been curious to learn more about Michael, but her in-laws rarely talked about him.

"I think it was just too painful for them to talk about Michael," Bernadette said. "I often wondered how Mark would be around the Campers. Would he be around the Campers even? That was a concern of mine. And now to see him with the Down syndrome Campers, I just—it makes me cry. Because he's so good with them. . . . I think Barnabas played a huge part in healing his heart."

Bernadette with Cyndy Teas

She smiled. "Who knew? Who knew that was going to be what came of it? I mean, this job has changed my nephew, my husband, my daughter. It's incredible."

Forever Friends

Though Bernadette's role has many emotionally heavy aspects to it, the parents' gratitude and the Campers' joy keep her going.

"These families are so thankful. I mean, just the gratitude on the phone, during drop-off: 'Thank you. Thank you, thank you, thank you for doing what you do.' When, you know, I love my job. And so for them to say thank you for doing something that blesses me? It's just, it's incredible."

As the only full-time medical Staff, Bernadette often receives emails with questions from Campers in the weeks leading up to Camp. Before the summer 2022 sessions began, she received an email from a young man named Bucky, who lives in Canada. The email exchanges that followed were a delight for her.

"He tells me he's nonverbal, but he uses a communication device, so he's typing. I loved my emails so much. I'm like, 'I can't wait to meet this person who's leaving Canada by himself, can't talk, in a wheelchair' . . . I'm like, 'That blows my mind.'"

When Bucky's week at Camp arrived, Bernadette looked forward to meeting him but hadn't yet had a chance to leave the Well House to go find him. Then she came out of her office to find a young man in a wheelchair waiting for her.

"He looked at my nametag, and he said, 'Bernadette,' and I looked at him, and he points at himself, and he says, 'Bucky, Bucky.' And I was like, 'Oh, my goodness.' I was so happy to meet him."

Bernadette has continued to stay in touch with Bucky. He is going to mail her some Canadian coffee, and she plans to send him homemade apple butter.

"I'm sure Bucky and I will be friends forever. But just being able to have these connections to make people more comfortable to come, that's so cool. That's my job. And I love that."

"[My first year], my mom was very nervous, and I was very nervous. I was scared of people picking me up and taking care of me, because at that point it had all been my mom and dad. . . . After the first year, you feel like you're at home here."

– Jansen W., Camper

CHAPTER 30

Story Builds Upon Story:
Debbie Weathermon, Parent and Development Director

As the mother to three older boys, Debbie Weathermon realized very early on that something was different about her fourth and youngest son, Jansen. Within a few months of his birth, she noticed he wasn't hitting certain physical milestones.

After many doctors' appointments, they finally found an answer: Jansen had had a stroke in utero and had cerebral palsy, which left him with very little mobility.

"Between the responsibilities of work and devoted care, the journey proved to be incredibly challenging," Debbie said. "Throughout the initial seven years of our child's life, he remained an inseparable part of our daily lives. We were fortunate to discover a wonderful daycare that could look after him while I was at work. However, finding additional assistance to allow us to have a moment for ourselves or spend quality time together was a struggle."

When Jansen was seven, Debbie and her husband, Jesse, took him to a doctor's appointment in St. Louis, and the doctor told them about Camp Barnabas. Intrigued, Debbie researched the Camp and then scheduled a tour.

"I went out [to Camp], and I'm in the golf cart [on a tour] . . . and he's on my lap and he's loving everything. Then something comes up about, 'Oh, it's overnight,' and I was like, 'Ohhh. No. I can't leave him overnight. There's no way.'"

But by the time summer came around, Debbie had worked up the courage to leave Jansen for a week.

"That first year, truly, I was terrified," she said. "I called all the time, wanting to know what he was doing, what he was eating. Like nonstop."

Debbie still distinctly remembers picking up Jansen that first summer. When he saw her coming, he burst into tears.

"I'm thinking, 'Oh my gosh, he must have missed me.' But as soon as I got closer, he's like, 'I don't want you here.' He was crying because I was there to pick him up and he wanted to stay."

Jansen at Camp

The realization of how much Camp meant to Jansen hit home.

"It was then that we realized that we had found this safe place for him. It was a place where no one was afraid of him. They weren't afraid to feed him. They weren't afraid to hang out with him. They weren't afraid to give him experiences. They loved him."

Jansen has gone to Camp Barnabas every summer since 2014. For Debbie and her family, that week has become a time to get away together.

"That week is truly a moment of respite, knowing that for one entire week, someone else is taking care of him. It's an unusual feeling to sit down for a meal and be able to eat without having to feed him too. Normally, every meal consists of me taking a bite, then giving him a bite, then taking another bite, and so on. So that one week where I can simply sit down and enjoy a meal becomes incredibly significant for me."

Genuine Friendships and a Bigger Mission

Jansen's stories from his time at Camp are never-ending. Debbie laughed as she admitted many of his stories are about things he was able to get away with, like sneaking out during rest time to go get ice cream. For him, it's a week to "hang out with the boys."

"I think the great thing for me as a parent of a Camper is to watch Jansen have true genuine friendships," Debbie said.

During Jansen's first summer at Camp, his Missionary was a teenager named Jack Sadler.[1] Jack continued to be Jansen's Missionary every year for nine years, and in 2022, he joined Barnabas Prep's year-long Fellow Program.

At a recent birthday party, Jansen invited a few friends from school, but everyone else on his invite list was from Camp Barnabas, including his most recent Missionary, Bethany, who lives in Dallas, Texas—more than a six-hour drive from the Weathermon home in Aurora, Missouri.

"She literally drove six hours to celebrate his birthday, and then turned around and drove back home that night—I think she got in at like two in the morning," Debbie said. "It's just a different feel out [at Camp Barnabas]. People are genuine and loving, and they pour into the Campers like nothing I've ever seen."

It was that type of genuine care that made Debbie interested in getting more involved. In 2018, Camp Barnabas held a meeting in Branson for anyone in the community who wanted to learn more about Barnabas. Debbie attended and heard about Barnabas Prep for the first time.

"I realized that it wasn't just a summer camp, that there is a whole other aspect to Barnabas and what they do," she said. "[Up until then] I was kind of that mom who just dropped my kid off and then came back and picked him up and knew he had the best time ever."

But listening to Barnabas's bigger mission touched Debbie's heart. While she was still sitting in the meeting, she texted her boss at the bank whom she'd worked with for more than ten years.

"I'm going to work for Barnabas," she said.

---

[1] Jack's story can be read in Chapter 23.

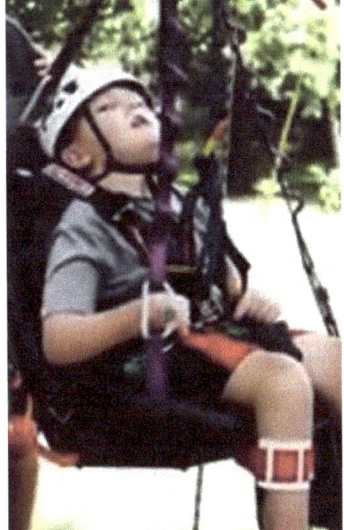

Jansen at Camp

"Come to my office and talk to me after you're done at the meeting," her boss texted back.

"So I did. I went back to her office, and she's just like, 'You are just so passionate about it.' She said, 'I would never hold you back.'"

Debbie reached out to Barnabas to let them know she was interested in working with them. About six months later, a position in development opened up, and Debbie applied and was hired.

"I'm going on five years now," she said. "It's incredible. I absolutely love it."

One of her favorite aspects of her job is getting to work in a faith-based environment.

"Barnabas is the first really Christian-based organization that I've worked for. Being at the bank, it was always a great environment and great organization," she said. "But [now] I love that there's constantly somebody pouring into you all the time. Like, every meeting starts with a prayer, every phone conversation starts with a prayer. I just think you live your life differently when you start everything in your day with the Lord. . . . It's brought me closer to the Lord, with my relationship with Him and just how I view people."

This is perhaps the biggest life lesson she's learned from her time at Barnabas.

"That's the only thing I would say is just continue to put Christ first."

Hidden Challenges

Debbie and Jesse have always worked to give Jansen a normal childhood experience.

"Jansen's always gotten in trouble just like his brothers got in trouble," she said. "He's been disciplined the same—we never treated him like he was in a chair."

That mindset means it's sometimes even harder for Jansen when strangers treat him differently.

"His biggest pet peeve is that people see a wheelchair, and they instantly talk to him like a baby," she said. "He'll go right back . . . and start talking to them like a baby, because it's so annoying to him. He's like, 'Just talk to me like I'm normal.'"

That would be her biggest advice to anyone who hasn't spent much time around people with disabilities—to realize they're people too and to treat them the same way they would anyone else.

Parenting a child with a disability entails many hidden challenges that often go unrecognized by those outside the disability community. Obtaining the necessary resources for Jansen proves to be an ongoing struggle, leaving no room for respite.

"The insurance company's decisions on what they deem medically necessary for my child add an additional layer of complexity to our already demanding journey," Debbie said. "We also often have to decline many well-intentioned

Jansen at Camp with Jack Sadler (right)

invitations to dinners or parties hosted at people's homes. Assessing accessibility becomes a constant concern, as we find ourselves unable to attend events in places with stairs or other barriers. Politely declining these invitations is done to avoid uncomfortable conversations about accessibility limitations. After so many declines, we quit being asked."

The loneliness this life sometimes involves is part of why Debbie appreciates the Barnabas community so much. Not only does it give her connections with other families who understand, but she also loves how Barnabas continually seeks innovative solutions to the various difficulties families face through things like Prep, scholarships, and weekend retreats.

Though being the parent of a child with a disability comes with many challenges, Debbie wouldn't change it.

"I love him more than anything and would never trade anything."

She doesn't think Jansen would change anything about his life either.

"If you ask Jansen, truthfully, he thinks he won the lottery by being disabled," she said. "He doesn't look at it as a disadvantage at all. He literally thinks he won the lottery, because he gets so much attention."

Telling the Story

As the development director at Barnabas, Debbie views her role as an incredible opportunity to share the impactful stories that unfold at Camp. She believes in the life-changing power of Barnabas, and she's driven to help more Campers, Students, and volunteers have those kinds of transformational experiences.

One heartwarming story came from the dad of a Missionary who called Debbie after his son returned home and shared how his son's life had been profoundly changed by his week at Camp. Eager to contribute, he asked Debbie about Camp's current needs.

"I took the chance to talk about the ongoing need for scholarships, which ease the financial burden for Campers' families, and shared our plans for a new dining hall," Debbie said.

Without hesitation, the man said, "You know, those all sound great to me. I'm going to send you a check for $200,000. You use it where it is most needed."

Debbie was blown away by his generosity. "He had never given to Barnabas before, but his son's experience made such a profound impact on him. But this story is not an isolated incident," she added. "I have been privileged to witness such incredible acts of kindness time and again. Last summer, we had two similar calls like this. People are truly incredible."

Debbie believes that the generosity she sees on a regular basis can be attributed to God using Camp to change people's lives.

"It comes back to the heart of Barnabas," she said. "It is a place where individuals, young and old, find transformation, hope, and purpose. I am constantly in awe of the generosity of people who wholeheartedly rally behind Barnabas's mission. Their unwavering support serves as a testament, reaffirming that the hand of God weaves through every step of Barnabas's transformative journey."

"It's like a little picture of heaven, a place where God uses everyone no matter where they're at. It's so beautiful to see Him at work here, as Missionaries arrive at Camp so nervous and [then] to be able to watch them grow in confidence and compassion as they get to know their Camper as a person. This place is unlike any place I've ever been, and it makes me yearn for heaven where all will be made new!"

– Christina S., Cabin Parent

CHAPTER 31

All Things New:
Jermaine Harrison, Youth Pastor

When Jermaine Harrison was growing up in Saint Martin, an island in the Caribbean, he had little idea of the journey God would take him on. Jermaine attended a small Baptist church throughout his childhood that he says fit every Baptist stereotype—pews, hymnals, King James Version, and all.

"I look back on it with great fondness, [because] that's where I placed my faith and trust in Jesus and knew that He was the Savior of the world," Jermaine said.

Toward the end of his high school years, Jermaine began to feel the Lord leading him toward full-time ministry.

"I didn't want it per se. But [God's direction] was clear and obvious through doors that were opening and doors that were closing."

Jermaine's calling led him to a small Bible college in the Virgin Islands and then to Dallas Theological Seminary to continue his education.

"So in the fall of 2010, I moved to Dallas, Texas, not knowing a soul, just on this journey, really one of faith and trust in the Lord and obedience to what I felt like He was leading me to do next."

About two years into seminary, Jermaine's car broke down, leaving him without a way to get to the church he had been attending. When one of his roommates invited him to his church, Watermark Community Church,[1] Jermaine decided to give it a try. Before long, Jermaine began volunteering with Watermark's student ministry. When he finished his seminary degree, he joined Watermark's staff for a one-year training program. Eventually, Jermaine moved up to men's coordinator and then high school director. Today, he's the director of the entire student ministry.

But before his career at Watermark took off, Jermaine had the chance to take part in one of the biggest service initiatives for the church's student ministry: spending a week at Camp Barnabas.

---

[1] www.watermark.org

Watermark students at Camp, Summer 2023

A Heart for Service

Watermark first got connected with Camp Barnabas in 2008. Rather than offering a fun summer camp on the beach, Jermaine's predecessors wanted to offer students a chance to serve in a way that would further their faith. Barnabas seemed like the perfect fit.

This proved to be true after only a few years of Watermark's youth serving at Camp Barnabas. At that point, Jermaine's bosses, David Penuel and Braun Brown, began looking for ways to go deeper and asked Camp Barnabas if there were any weeks that were harder to staff. The answer came that Week Four in late June, which primarily welcomed Campers with disabilities related to mobility, was often a tough one to staff. So Watermark began bringing a large team every summer during Week Four.

"I think the heart was, if we're going to serve, why not go all in and serve where the need is greatest?" Jermaine explained.

During Jermaine's first summer at Camp in 2014, he served as a Cabin Dad for a group of eighth and ninth grade Barnstormers—younger students who serve food in the dining hall and help tidy up the cabins. He loved getting to see those students dipping their feet in the water of service, as they prepared to one day be Camp Missionaries. He also loved watching students learn to serve in obscurity.

"No one's looking behind there and seeing you washing all the dishes or taking the trash out necessarily. And you know, it's not the most, like, sexy thing to go back home and say, 'Hey, I was washing dishes literally for six days straight.' But it just teaches you to have a heart of service, whether it's recognized or not, and also to see how little things matter a ton—like literally, if we didn't do any of that, the Campers wouldn't be able to have the experience that they have," he said. "And truly, I feel like that experience has even helped me in my position as the director of our student ministry here, after all these years of being on staff, just to learn . . . that the little things matter."

Over time, the connection between Watermark and Camp Barnabas has turned into a strong, long-lasting relationship—as have the relationships between Watermark staff and many Campers.

"What I've seen [as I'm] about to go on my ninth summer now at Camp Barnabas is the blessing of continual relationships. One of the highlights for me is . . . to see the same Campers year after year, and build relationships with them, man, has been such an incredible joy."

Jermaine always looks forward to seeing a Camper named Carter, who uses a wheelchair and isn't able to communicate much verbally. Jermaine has enjoyed building a relationship with him through the years.

"It is so cool to see how excited he gets about Camp. . . . When we're eating lunch or a meal, the Campers can go up to the front and sing a song. And we'll always be like, 'Carter, you want to sing a song?' And he always wants to sing a song." Jermaine smiled. "To just see the joy on his face and to see that, while he may not have the same mental faculties as me, he remembers me, you know, or he remembers us from all the years before. When we come back this summer, and he sees us, he's gonna remember us, and he's gonna be so happy to see us, and we're gonna be so happy to see him. And so, man, those long-term relationships are really, really sweet."

A Ripple Effect

Over Jermaine's ten years of involvement in Watermark's student ministry, he has seen student after student impacted by their time at Camp. Every month, Watermark hosts a gathering for all their high school students to worship together, and each month, a student shares a five-minute testimony of how God is working in their lives. Many times, those testimonies include stories about how God used Camp Barnabas to open the students' eyes to the needs of the world around them and to help them understand the gospel more clearly. Many students have also gone on to work at Camp Barnabas or to pursue a career working with the disability community.

Jermaine described one family with four kids who have all served at Camp, one after the other. The oldest is now twenty-four.

"I remember being at Camp with him as his Cabin Dad in one of his years during high school, and . . . he would come back home and tell his siblings, 'This is an amazing experience. You've got to try it.' One by one they would try it. So now the youngest of the four kids is a senior, and she's going to be working there all summer. And then her brother, who is just finishing his freshman year in college, is also going to be working on Staff there this summer," Jermaine said. "There's dozens of stories like that where students would go, have an experience that really touched their hearts or challenged them to view the world differently, and then go out and serve."

Watermark has a ministry for people with disabilities called Kaleidoscope. Jermaine has noticed that some of the students who go to Camp Barnabas in the summers return home and want to serve with Kaleidoscope.

"They're like, 'Hey, I don't want to just do it this one week for the year. I want to be able to serve and contribute at other times.' So we have numerous kids . . . giving care to people with special and additional needs here in our church and making them feel included and welcome as well."

Jermaine has been amazed how quickly communication barriers disappear between his students and Campers throughout their week together. At the start of the week, students sometimes struggle to understand Campers who may communicate by using hand signs, pointing to symbols or illustrations on a communication board, and a variety of other mannerisms. But by the middle of the week, that struggle has typically disappeared.

"It's like they've learned a whole new language . . . it's so easy for them," Jermaine said. "It doesn't take that long to overcome the nervousness or intimidation or feeling of inadequacy that you might have caring for or having a relationship with someone with special and additional needs."

Growth and Grief

Personally, Jermaine says Camp Barnabas has helped him grow in his ability to live and lead in a more patient and caring way.

"I've learned to just grow in empathy, humility, patience, just from the experience, whether that be encouraging and coaching and shepherding our kids, or getting on the ground in a cabin with a Camper who's struggling with something, or just helping with a transfer to the bathroom or helping a Camper go get their shower, something like that," he said. "No one's ever accused me of being a gentle soul, per se, and I feel like I've just learned so much about humility and gentleness and patience and compassion—just as a follower of Jesus from going and serving over the course of this week."

For Jermaine and many of his fellow staff members, serving at Camp Barnabas each year has also become a sweet reminder of the joy awaiting them in heaven. He imagines sitting around a dinner table, feasting in heaven, with many of the Campers they've built relationships with.

"Isn't it amazing to think that there's going to be literally hundreds of Camp Barnabas Campers who will be there with us in heaven and [that we'll get] to communicate verbally with Campers we had relationships with for years and years but weren't ever able to communicate with in that way? Or to see them walking and running? I mean, it's just gonna be a big party," Jermaine said. "We love thinking about that and longing for that and longing for the day when their bodies—and our bodies—are all made new by the power of Jesus."

Watermark students at Camp, Summer 2023

In 2017, that reminder that all things will be restored became particularly poignant for the Watermark staff and families in an extremely difficult way.

Austin Silva, one of Watermark's high school students who Jermaine described as well-liked by everyone, a leader among the students, and a former Missionary at Camp Barnabas, went to the doctor for a routine wisdom teeth extraction. Later that day, Watermark staff received word that Austin was in the hospital after medical errors related to his procedure and was fighting for his life. Ten days later, he passed away.

What followed was one of the most difficult periods of Watermark's student ministry.

"For that entire week [that he was in the hospital], we were up at the hospital every day, just kind of waiting and praying and encouraging students," Jermaine said. "It was really, really hard."

The day that Austin passed away happened to fall just a few days before Watermark was due to head to Camp Barnabas for the week. The staff was torn over whether to cancel the trip but ultimately made the decision to go. Camp Barnabas had greatly impacted Austin's faith, so the trip felt like a meaningful way to honor him. Additionally, the staff knew that a week of serving at Camp would provide the students with time to process Austin's passing together. The week that followed was full of bittersweet moments.

"It was just a very heavy and emotional time for our ministry and all our students. They have a cross at Camp Barnabas with the names of different Campers who have [passed away] and people who are associated with Camp who've passed away. That summer, we got to put his name—Austin Silva's name—up on the cross. And, man, it was heavy, it was emotional, and it was one of the hardest times for our student ministry."

For Jermaine, who was in the hospital room with Austin not long before he passed, the reminder that he would see Austin again one day became something he clung to.

"One day . . . we'll get to rejoice over the time that we were here on earth together," Jermaine said. "[That's something] that comes to my mind when I think about how the Lord has used Camp and used the experience to just show us more of who He is, and to remind us that this world isn't our home, and that one day, He's going to make all things new. He will. There'll be no more wheelchairs, there'll be no more mental disabilities, or anything else. But [we'll] all be clear-minded and free and whole with Him in Heaven. And I can't wait."

When Jermaine considers the future of Watermark's student ministry, he can't imagine Camp Barnabas not being a part of it.

"We do a lot of fun things. We do a lot of big things, as you could imagine, like retreats or different events that are well produced with great communication of God's Word. Those things are right and good, and we're going to continue to do them. But if all else fails, and there's only a few things that we can do, as long as Camp Barnabas is an option, I don't see why we wouldn't do it. The opportunity to see the gospel, share the gospel, live the gospel, experience the gospel, grow and be challenged in your faith, serve someone else—I mean, literally, it's so much of what God's Word has to say. . . . Why wouldn't we take advantage of this amazing experience and opportunity to serve others just like Christ came to serve us?"

"[Camp Barnabas] has made me realize that working with people with special needs is a calling for me and that I want to do it more often."

– Sydney S., Missionary

CHAPTER 32

Deeply Rooted Passion:
Caroline Tillack, Summer Staff and Development Specialist

When Caroline Tillack was in sixth grade, two boys with disabilities became her best friends. One had an undiagnosed disability involving a developmental delay, while the other had sustained brain damage from the abuse he suffered as a young child before being adopted from Russia.

"Every day I would sit by them, every day I'd play at recess with them—they were my guys." Caroline smiled. "It was so neat, because I look back at that year of my life, and I see how the Lord was planting seeds of passion in my heart for the special needs community and ultimately directing my path."

On the last day of sixth grade, she said goodbye to the boys for the summer and then climbed into the car with her mom.

"Caroline, I think you need to go into something that deals with disability ministry or become a special education teacher," her mom said.

"Yeah, maybe," Caroline replied.

While her passion for people with disabilities was undeniable, it would be years before Caroline decided to turn that passion into a career.

"During my first year of college, I kept pushing aside my passion for special needs. I was so aware of how much the Lord had given me, and because of that I was determined not to live a mediocre life for Christ. In my mind, that meant that I needed to go into the most challenging career—not sure where that idea came from." She laughed.

Caroline started college in pre-med in 2018 but very quickly realized it was not a good fit. Around the same time, her family got very involved with Barnabas Prep. The Students began spending a lot of time at the Tillack home, and Caroline also spent a week at Camp Barnabas as a Missionary that summer. All those experiences reignited her passion for working with people with disabilities.

"Fortunately, by the time I started my sophomore year of college, I feel like the Lord told me that obedience is excellence in His eyes, and for me that meant being obedient to the call of working with individuals with special needs. I am

Caroline with a Camper

so thankful for the Lord's patience with me while I was praying . . . and weeping to Him as I was failing my way through Chemistry 101 my freshman year. He was kind to direct me back to what I love and to the people I love."

Since that time, Caroline has held a variety of roles at Barnabas, including Summer Staff, where she was assigned to a cabin of Campers each week for the summer, and cabin supervisor, where she led other women on Staff. As part of the cabin supervisor role, she and others on the cabin supervisor team also worked with Campers who were struggling to adapt to their week at Camp. After her summer on the leadership team at Camp, she became the Barnabas development team's intern, which allowed her to use her new degree in public relations and advertising. Most recently, Caroline came on full time with Barnabas as a development specialist.

Caroline said that her time spent working on the cabin supervisor team was the best and most rewarding summer of her life. It wasn't easy by any means, but Caroline loved every aspect of the job.

"What made that role on Summer Staff so special was that we got to see Campers start their week having a lot of really challenging behaviors, but by the end of the week, they would be going down the slides at the pool having the time of their lives. The job felt like a puzzle in a way. With every Camper who had challenges behaviorally, we would ask ourselves the question of, 'OK, how can I help you succeed?' And, 'What plan can we put in place that will help you have the best week of your life?'"

When she has her development hat on, she loves building relationships and sharing with people about what the Lord is doing through Barnabas, but her sweet spot is when she gets to be out at Camp for a day and talk with Campers.

She smiled. "Let me hang out with Campers, and I'm in heaven."

The Gift of Rest

One story stands out from Caroline's time working as a cabin supervisor. For her, it highlighted the critical respite that Camp Barnabas provides to families. As part of her role, Caroline got the opportunity to call many of the families beforehand to learn more about the Campers who would be attending that summer. One mother turned out to be the mom of not just one Camper, but three.

Through their conversation, the mom not only shared all that Camp needed to know about her three kids, but she also shared part of her story with Caroline.

For a long time, this woman and her husband had struggled with infertility. They decided to try IVF and ended up pregnant with four babies. At the time of birth, only three of the babies survived, and all three were eventually diagnosed with cerebral palsy. Additionally, during the process of the pregnancy and babies' birth, things shifted between the woman and her husband, and she was soon faced with the reality of raising three children with severe disabilities as a single mom.

When Caroline talked to this mom, the triplets—two girls and a boy—were eight years old. They all used wheelchairs and had few communication abilities. Each of the Campers has a variety of specific needs and challenges that their mom began to list off during the conversation, such as feeding tubes, special sleeping arrangements to avoid harm, braces, behavioral challenges, etc. The mom was faithful in her love and care for them but was also looking forward to the week of rest that Camp Barnabas would offer.

"As soon as she came to drop off her three kids at Camp, everyone on Staff, the Missionaries, other parents were all in awe at what a powerhouse this wom-

Caroline with a Camper

Caroline with a Campers

an was," Caroline explained. "She was on her own and one by one unloaded each child out of the car and did it all. . . . She does it all by herself every single day. We were all just blown away."

In their phone call, the mom had explained to Caroline the emotional weight of caring for all her children by herself. Thankfully, she had a good community to support her, but ultimately, their care fell to her. Before sending her kids to Camp, she hadn't had a night to herself since they were born.

"Our medical director once asked this mom what she was going to do with her week [while her kids were at Camp]. She was like, 'I'm bringing my camper to the woods, and I'm just going to sit in my trailer and rest.' . . . Honestly, I think it's more of a gift to the mom than even the kids—the kids will have fun no matter what. But you see and can imagine how exhausted she must be, and it is one of the greatest feelings to know that we were able to spend a week with her kids while she got to take a break."

Loving Like Jesus

After about five years of involvement with Camp Barnabas, Caroline still finds herself surprised by the ways it continues to transform her life.

"I think coming into Barnabas, I thought I was patient and had a servant's heart. But after my first day as a missionary, I quickly realized that I was nowhere near as patient or servant hearted as I thought. Serving at Camp Barnabas tests your patience and your selflessness at a whole other level. I feel like growth, sanctification, and overall sharpening is expedited at Barnabas because it's so focused on others."

When Caroline was growing up, her dad always taught her and her siblings to do the opposite of their flesh. In other words, do the opposite of what a sinful, selfish nature would urge.

"Working at Camp also put this to the test. My flesh wants to serve myself first, but at Camp you have no choice but to do the opposite of your flesh and serve others, which ultimately means walking in the leading of the Holy Spirit.

"I couldn't imagine going to Camp and not being a Christian, because every time I make a decision or do the opposite of my flesh, it's not because of me. If I didn't have Christ inside of me [or wasn't] abiding in Christ, my flesh would win."

Caroline views Camp as an opportunity for Missionaries to let Christ love the Campers through them.

"Whenever we love the Campers, it's not an empty love of 'Hey, let's be best friends.' We can truly speak life and purpose and encouragement into their lives with love that actually has weight, because it's the love of Jesus," she emphasized.

That seed of passion for working with people with disabilities that was planted when Caroline was in sixth grade continues to grow. Today, she counts several people with disabilities as some of her closest friends.

"Some of the Campers and Students at Barnabas Prep who I have gotten to know over the past five years are in the running for a bridesmaid in my future wedding."

Her passion for people with disabilities goes hand-in-hand with her walk with God.

"Some people say, 'Oh, when I'm on top of a mountain or at the ocean, I feel close to the Lord.' I'm like, 'When I'm at Barnabas, I feel closer to God.' . . . My time at Barnabas and the many hours spent with individuals who have every reason to be sad or have a bad attitude but choose to live joyfully has only propelled my love for Jesus and desire to walk faithfully with Him."

"There's no need to go halfway across the world to find a need. The need is here. If what you're looking for is the formation of character and compassion and empathy, this is a super-concentrated dose of formation."

– Troy F., Physician Assistant

CHAPTER 33

A Perfect Opportunity:
Dr. Jake Spain, Doctor

Sometime in 2018, Dr. Jake Spain and his wife, Pam, started praying for a volunteer opportunity that would allow them to serve as a family and Jake to use his medical skills. It was a hard combination to find.

Then they ran into one of Jake's former coworkers at a coffee shop. She told them she was working at Camp Barnabas, which was in need of more doctors to volunteer each week during the summer. As she shared, Jake realized this could be exactly what he and his family were looking for.

As an emergency medicine physician, Jake worried a little whether his skills would be a good fit for what Barnabas needed. He wondered if a PM&R (physical medicine and rehabilitation) doctor would be better, but he hoped he could still be helpful. He signed up to volunteer in the summer of 2019 and quickly found his worries to be unfounded.

"I got there, and it turns out, it's all emergency medicine," he said. "I mean this is perfect—it couldn't be a better match for who they need there. When I got there, I was like, 'Oh, this is exactly what I do every day.'"

He loved the chance to use his skills for the benefit of others instead of getting caught up in all the "extra" stuff that working in a hospital requires.

"It's an opportunity to do medicine for the sake of doing medicine. You're doing medicine just to be helpful . . . it takes you back to the enjoyment of doing what you do to help others," he said. "I mean, I enjoy what I do on a daily basis, and as a career, it's great for me, but what we do [at Camp Barnabas] feels amazing."

His family loved it too. Pam volunteers in the Well House, doing odd jobs and serving wherever she's needed. Their tween daughter, Kate, has attended Camp through the Sibling Program once or twice, but other weeks, she has hung out in the Well House instead, often accompanying the nurses as they distribute medicine to Campers.

"My family was really re-energized by [serving] and felt like we absolutely had to come back. It was just very, very obvious that we were going to be coming back again."

Jake, Pam, and Kate Spain

Unexpected Lessons

Though Jake and his family have been coming to Camp Barnabas for only a few years, he's already had multiple interactions with Missionaries, Campers, and families that have had a lasting impact on him.

One was with a quiet seventeen-year-old Missionary who was assigned to a Camper who used a wheelchair and had very limited communication abilities. The Camper had a rough week physically, including several seizures. Toward the end of the week, Jake spotted the Missionary pushing the Camper back and forth in his wheelchair. Jake took a moment to talk with him, figuring he must be exhausted.

"Man, I bet you are excited to get some rest tomorrow," Jake said to the Missionary. "You did a great job this week. . . . I'm sure you're just exhausted and looking forward to getting home."

"Actually, I really want to talk to [my Camper's] guardian tomorrow," the Missionary said. "It's been an amazing week. It was such an honor to get to take care of him. It really challenged my faith, and I really grew a ton. . . . I just want to tell his dad thanks so much. Like, that was such an awesome blessing to get to be with him all week long."

Jake was caught off-guard by the Missionary's enthusiasm.

"Yes, you should talk to his dad," Jake replied. "That is fantastic."

Pam overheard the conversation, and afterward, she and Jake could only look at each other, tears welling up over the unexpected moment.

"That's one of my favorite stories of this year," Jake said. "I don't think that father probably ever imagined that his son [who was nonverbal and] in a wheelchair would help minister to a young kid over a week and grow his faith."

Jake mentioned another interaction with a Camper that taught him never to make assumptions about someone's level of understanding or ability to communicate. He had made a rule for himself to speak with all Campers in the same way he would with anyone else, regardless of what their disability appeared to be. During a quiet moment, he sat down next to a Camper in a wheelchair, smiled, and asked how she was enjoying the week. Based on the Camper's more noticeable physical disabilities, he wasn't expecting an answer. But given a little time and patience, the Camper began telling him about her week at Camp and her upcoming plans to travel to her brother's wedding.

"We had a pleasant, pleasant time. It was one of my favorite interactions with a Camper, actually, [that] whole summer."

The realization of how incorrect his first assumption had been hit Jake hard.

"It was like, this little light went off," he explained. "I mean, it was one of those moments where I was almost embarrassed—like, how many opportunities have I missed in my life? I told my wife, 'Oof, that one got me.' I now take [my rule] so much more seriously."

High Stakes

Working in the Well House means that Jake sees some of the harder, more serious aspects of Camp too.

"We say yes to a really big group of high-risk people . . . a lot of these people are in the hospital multiple times a year. If you take them for a week in the

Jake and Kate at a pool party at Camp

summer, you're likely going to get somebody [out of] thousands of Campers who need[s] to go to the hospital," he said. "[Camp Barnabas does] it really carefully, really wisely . . . I've never seen [getting additional] care be delayed . . . but I say that just so people understand the stakes are high. [The Campers are] real people's loved ones and have really, really high needs and are very sick a lot of the time. They have conditions that leave them in the hospital monthly, often more than that during rough times. So it's real-deal care that we're giving there. It's not just splinters and sunburns."

Jake has seen both the beautiful and the hard sides of that at Barnabas. One fun moment for him was when he sat in on a call with a Camper's parents along with Bernadette Losh, Camp Barnabas's health services director.[1]

"The parents said, 'Hey, we're sending our daughter, but we want to make sure that you guys can take her, that you're really OK with this,'" Jake remembered.

They outlined their daughter's needs: She had a rare genetic disorder, her intestines were failing, and she took all her feedings through an IV.

"We listened to it all, and I kind of looked at Bernadette. I was like, 'Absolutely, yeah.' We were all in agreement. We're all kind of nodding. We're like, 'Yeah, we can absolutely take care of it. This is not a problem at all. It's very much within what we can do.' I think the parents were just shocked. They're like, 'Really?' We're like, 'Yeah, absolutely.'

"I think this is the ministry of Barnabas, is being able to take . . . the Campers who would otherwise be told no," Jake explained. "That's why Barnabas is really cool, because no one else offers that. It was really fun to be on the phone and be able to say, 'Of course,' and hear this family very excited and the Camper be very excited. And she actually came to Camp and had an amazing experience."

---

[1] Bernadette's story can be read in Chapter 29.

Missionary worship session before orientation

Jake also shared a sobering conversation he had with the guardian of a Camper who was on hospice. The Camper was struggling physically during her week at Camp, especially with her oxygen levels. Jake called the guardian to see what she wanted to do.

"I know she's on hospice," he said. "Do you want us to take her to a hospital? We certainly could."

The guardian was quiet for a moment. "You know, if she dies at Barnabas, that is her favorite place on earth. I want her to be able to experience Barnabas. So if you can help come up with a plan, I'd like her to stay there if possible."

Jake agreed immediately. "She's on hospice—it makes a lot of sense. I totally understand that decision."

They came up with a plan to increase a few of the Camper's medications and to try having her sleep sitting up to see if it helped increase her oxygen levels. The next morning, Jake woke up early, threw on his shoes, and went to check on the Camper.

"I got one of the female Staff Members [to come with me]. I run over there to check on her, just hoping she's doing OK," he said. "We open the door and walk in the cabin. And she's doing great. She did great sitting up in bed while sleeping, and her oxygen was good. I was so excited for her, and so we ended the week successfully."

Later that year, Jake and Pam happened to see that Camper at an event in their hometown of Springfield, Missouri.

"My wife looks at me, and I'm like, 'Yes. That's her.' And she started crying . . . 'She's still alive.'" He smiled. "She was doing actually better than last year, which was really cool. But it was a huge moment for us, just as volunteers. You get very emotionally involved, and we were so excited that she was doing so well."

It's a story he's sometimes hesitant to share, even though it's one that stands out to him.

"I'm always nervous to share that story, just because I don't know if everybody quite understands the balance that you have with hospice and that it was a loving thing that guardian was trying to give her [by] not taking her away from [that experience] when she knew that she was going to probably still have the same problems at home [if she left]," Jake said. "But I understood it was an empathetic decision from her guardian—it was not a careless one."

The Joy of Serving

In 2021, Barnabas's board members were looking for another doctor, preferably one from Springfield, to join the board, and they asked Jake to consider the role. He was honored to accept.

"Board positions are kind of the shiny penny," he said. "We get a lot of recognition . . . but everyone else is doing the hard stuff. We show up and smile

Opening night at the lake

and are like, 'Yeah, sure, let's build that. That'd be great. Yeah, let's approve that.' I don't think it's a whole lot of work for us, but it's a lot of fun."

Jake has loved using his medical expertise and his role on the board to help improve the quality of care the Well House is able to offer. For example, he recently worked with Bernadette to put together emergency medical bags.

"It was really fun—like, 'Oh, this medical bag, I can make this way better... Let's find the right thing so that if you do have an emergency, you know where everything is, what you need, and you have it all right there.'"

He has also worked with his hospital to get at-cost medications for the Well House, helping to ensure its pharmacy is fully stocked.

"That was where I really had a lot of fun and still do. I still really enjoy the equipment side and getting everything set up."

That enjoyment still can't quite compare to the joy of volunteering at Barnabas in the summers though.

"It feels great," he said. "We thought it'd be really hard to take a week off, and then we [realized] it was difficult, but we could do it. Then we did two weeks, and I thought two weeks would be super hard. I was like, 'I don't know how we're gonna fit two weeks into our schedules. . . . We'll just have to figure it out,' and we did it. Now we've done two weeks, and it felt *so* good this year that I've been wanting to do three. Now I'm like, 'Can we do this for a month? Or can we figure out a way to do it one week a month?' So it feels great. It feels really, really good."

"Camp Barnabas is freedom from the social norms and expectations of the world and is a place that Campers and Missionaries get to feel loved and accepted."

– Kendall B., Missionary

CHAPTER 34

Rest and Belonging:
Jenn and Tyler Moore, Parents

For Jenn and Tyler Moore's family, the path to Camp Barnabas started with a Facebook post in 2016.

Jenn was scrolling through social media when she saw a picture of a young Chinese boy along with a blog post written by an orphanage. Her friend who had shared the link wrote, "I would love for one of my friends to become his forever family."

Something about the boy's picture struck Jenn. A quiet whisper entered her heart: "This is your son."

Jenn and her husband, Tyler, had briefly considered adoption five years earlier when their doctor advised them not to have any more kids after baby number three. But they could never quite get on the same page—Tyler wanted to adopt an older child, and Jenn wanted to adopt a baby—so they'd set the topic aside and hadn't given it much thought since. So when Jenn felt the Lord's prompting over the Facebook post, she was floored.

"I was like, 'Really? Where did that even come from?' So I clicked the link and read the blog post, and I just—I just lost it. I just kind of knew in that moment that [adopting him] was what the Lord wanted for us."

When Tyler came home, Jenn met him at the door in tears. "I need you to read this," she said, handing him the phone.

Tyler remembers thinking that he needed to leave and come back in. "I wasn't sure what I was walking into."

After reading the blog post, Tyler just looked at Jenn. "OK, so what are you thinking?"

"I think the Lord is really calling us to adopt this little boy," she replied. "I think we need to at least think about it."

Though Tyler wasn't as sure as Jenn was, he agreed to explore the idea. They reached out to the adoption agency to find out what would be required to adopt this boy. In the process, they were told that he was nine years old (they would later learn he was actually closer to seven) and that he had cerebral palsy.

Jenn and Tyler with Finley

Tyler admits it took a long time for him to become convinced this was the right decision for their family.

"It sounded like I walked in the door, and she handed me her phone, and it was happy ever after. It really was more [like], 'Well, I'm so thankful that you feel like God spoke to you, but I haven't heard anything,'" he remembered. "It was that way for several months. Like, 'OK, what is this about? I'm not there.'"

About five or six months into the adoption process, Tyler gained clarity while spending time with God early one morning.

"I feel like God said, 'Hey, who did I tell first about Jesus? Joseph or Mary?' And I was like, 'Oh, I think he actually told Mary first.' So it was kind of like that started breaking down that wall, started helping me understand where we were headed."

God provided several more confirmations over the next few months, including the revelation that their soon-to-be son, Finley, was able to climb stairs, despite his cerebral palsy. This came as a relief, because the Moores had recently bought a new house that only had upstairs bedrooms and had just been discussing a few days earlier how in the world it would work to have a son with cerebral palsy use an upstairs bedroom.

"We just kept having those kinds of confirmations along the way," Tyler said.

A Challenging Transition

It took eleven months from beginning to end for the Moores to bring Finley home. But unlike many of the idealistic endings to adoption stories found in books and movies, Jenn and Tyler found that completing the adoption launched them into a storm of dealing with the trauma and abandonment Finley had suffered. To make matters worse, they didn't speak Mandarin, Finley's native language, and he didn't speak English.

"Just everyday was a battle, four or five hours of just screaming, crying," Tyler said.

Over time, they learned more of Finley's story. He had never known his dad, but he had lived with his mom up until he was about five years old.

"He remembers a man coming the night before [and spending] the night with them, and the next day, they went and got on a train," Tyler said. "They were on the train for a while. We don't know how far that train [traveled], because he did not speak the same dialect of the people where they were when they found him.... [His mom and the man] sat him on another chair across the aisle from them. He fell asleep. When he woke up, she was gone, and he could see that man further down the train, but he wouldn't come to his help. That's how he was abandoned. He remembers all of it."

Jenn and Tyler leaned on counselors, social workers, and other friends who had adopted to support them as they helped Finley work through the trauma of losing his birth mom. In addition, their entire family also faced the challenge of learning about cerebral palsy.

One lesson was that spontaneity was no longer possible. Making sure the places they visit are accessible takes careful planning. Welcoming a child with a

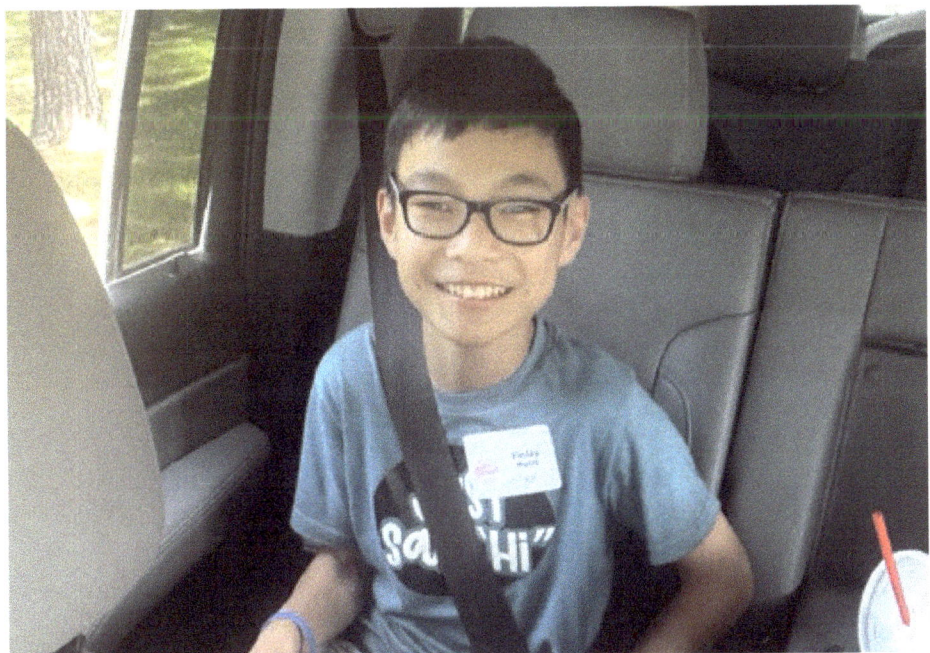

Finley on the way to Camp

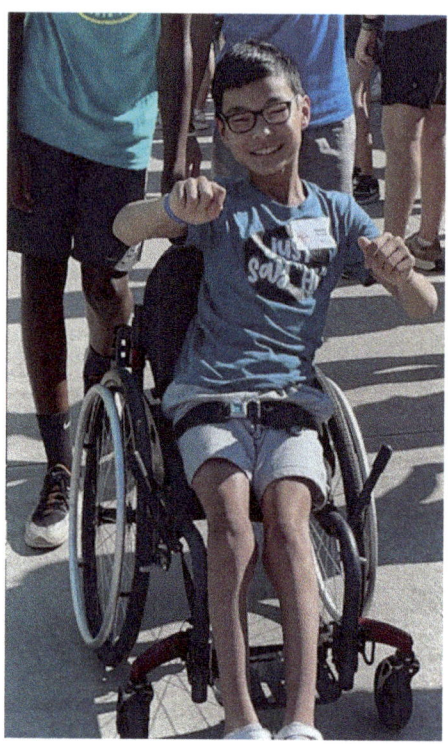

Finley at Camp

disability into their family also meant dealing with changes to the way strangers interacted with them.

"Specifically at church ... people just want to come and make [Finley] feel really welcome," Tyler said. "They're doing everything right. They're doing all the right things, but they'll walk up and totally go, 'Hey, how do I meet you?' [to Finley]. 'What's your name?' And you'll go, 'Oh, and by the way, [these are my] other kids.' And they go, 'Oh, OK, great.' And so your kids feel less than."

The transition for their three biological children hasn't always been easy.

"They sacrifice too, quite a bit, and they don't know how to express that to people, so it gets overlooked a lot,'" Tyler said. "But I think it's also ... been really eye-opening for them in that way, just in being inconvenienced, and having to really come out of yourself and then do something for someone else ... it teaches empathy."

Jenn agreed. "They're still brothers and sisters, and they still are crabby with each other, and they fight like brothers and sisters.... But they'll be the first one to take up for him. If they feel like an injustice is being done, they'll come to his defense really quickly."

One of the saddest things for Jenn is the loneliness she sometimes sees in Finley. He's friendly and funny, so people are drawn to him, and they're often curious about his disability, she explained. But the friendships don't always go deeper.

"He never has a sleepover. He never has friends who invite him to come play. He went all summer without one friend," she said. "And so that is hard—I think that to me is harder than any physical aspect ... when your kid says that he's lonely. . . . He's just a kid like every other kid. He wants to play. It's just—I wish people knew that kids with disabilities are just kids. They just maybe can't do the same things, but they still want friendships. They still want to have sleepovers. They still want to be invited to birthday parties."

It was in the middle of some of the upheaval their family was facing that the Moores first learned about Camp Barnabas. There, they found an answer to many of the challenges they faced shortly after Finley's adoption.

A Place to Belong

In late 2017, the Moores attended a cerebral palsy conference in Dallas hosted by Finley's doctor. As they wandered through the vendor booths, one caught their attention—Camp Barnabas.

At the time, Finley had only been with their family for a few months, and they didn't think it would be good to send him to Camp for a week yet. But early on the next year, they began talking up Camp Barnabas to Finley.

"We [told him], 'It's gonna be so much fun. You're gonna have so much fun'—but in the back of our minds, we were like, 'Oh, man, I hope he can handle it. Oh, man, I hope it is gonna be fun. I hope we get a week and not just like . . . eight hours,'" Jenn remembered. "The first night, they called and said that he had a tummy ache. And I said, 'OK,' and so I think we did get to talk to him. I said, 'You know, you probably have a tummy ache because you're away from home, but you know what, you're gonna have so much fun, and we miss you, and we love you, and we're close by, and we'll see you on Friday.' After that, we never heard another thing. We were just waiting for that next phone call, and it just never came. And yeah, [when] we picked him up, he'd had so much fun. It was just such a relief, because we thought, 'OK, well, this can be our thing every year.'"

The next year COVID-19 hit, and Camp was canceled. Then in 2021, the Moores checked out another camp for kids with disabilities in Colorado. But at the end of that week, Finley said he liked Camp Barnabas best.

"We were like, 'That's it. . . . That's what we're doing from now on,'" Jenn said. "So that just really solidified it for us. It just felt like that was a little second home."

Tyler distinctly remembers a story that Barnabas CEO John Tillack[1] told at a Barnabas fundraising event. For Tyler, the story underlines the gift that Camp Barnabas offers to parents. When John was about ten years old, he and his dad went fishing in a yellow canoe in the early hours of the morning before it was light out. A rustling noise in the middle of the lake caught their attention. When they went to investigate, they found a disoriented black Labrador, who'd lost track of the shore and was paddling for his life.

They hauled the dog into the boat. His muzzle was covered with the silver hairs of an aging dog, and he was clearly exhausted. He lay in the bottom of the boat for an hour, barely moving. John wasn't sure he was going to survive, but after they fed him a couple bologna sandwiches and gave him some water, the Lab began to revive. Then the dog spotted a flock of ducks splashing nearby, and in an instant, he leapt back into the water.

"Dad, he's gonna die!" John said.

"No, that dog just needed a break," John's dad replied. "That's what dogs do."

---

[1] John's story can be read in Chapter 26.

In his talk, John compared Barnabas to the yellow canoe—a safe place that provides families of people with disabilities a chance to rest before diving back into the often-exhausting realities of daily life.

"That story hit home so much," Tyler said. "Parents, when they drop [their kids] off, every single one of them takes a big, giant, deep breath. The first time we dropped [Finley] off . . . we had everyone in the car, and it's like, we all needed to know that he was going to be taken care of and that he was going to have a blast. And it's like, as soon as we dropped him off, our whole family just exhaled."

For Tyler and Jenn, these two things are equally important: that their family gets a chance to rest and that Finley gets to go somewhere fun and safe where he knows he belongs.

Finley's first year at Camp, he didn't try too many of the activities, but during his second year, he tried everything—ziplining, fishing, swimming, and more.

"I think he just overall enjoys the heck out of it," Tyler said. "I love the cause, I love the Camp, and I'm so thankful that we have that for him to look forward to and for us to look forward to, because that's a big deal."

Jenn loves that the loneliness and the sense of not fitting in that Finley sometimes feels at home doesn't apply at Camp Barnabas.

"He gets to go to Camp Barnabas and not worry about that," she said. "That's the one place he just feels at home, and he feels comfortable, and he feels like he belongs. That is super important, to feel like you belong somewhere."

A Continuing Story

Jenn and Tyler say their family is still learning, still growing through the challenges that come with adoption and disabilities, but they feel like their family has taken some huge strides forward.

"We had, I'm gonna say, three years of just massive upheaval in our house, emotional upheaval," Tyler said. "I think we both felt like we went through a major loss in our family. . . . We're going on year six in August. And I mean, we have turned a major corner, I think. Major corner. It probably took four years to turn that corner."

A few years after Jenn and Tyler adopted Finley, a memory came back to Tyler. When he and Jenn first started talking about getting married and having kids, Tyler had a gut feeling that God was going to give them a child with a disability.

"I didn't even remember that until last year, five years after it happened," Tyler said. "I just think that's really kind of interesting . . . you just can't ever put God in a box, and you can't ever get in front of God, because His plans are bigger than ours.

"Everybody goes through things in their life and you kind of watch and wonder, 'How's God gonna do this?' . . . I don't know. I just know the story's not done… [I know] that God is working on every single one of us in a completely different way, even Finn."

Afterword:
Embracing the Extraordinary Journey of Barnabas

As I reflect upon the stories shared in this book, I am overwhelmed by a profound sense of gratitude and wonder. The journey we took through these pages was one of endless inspiration, unwavering resilience, and genuine human connection.

From the laughter that echoes throughout Camp to the heartfelt conversations on Prep's campus, we witnessed the power of unity—where differences were not merely tolerated but celebrated. I love how each story reveals that disabilities are not barriers to be overcome, but rather facets of identity that add richness to our lives. The strength of character displayed by Campers, Missionaries, Students, Staff, families, and board members alike illuminates the boundless potential that exists within the human spirit.

Through my time working here, I have come to see Barnabas as a haven of acceptance and a sanctuary of belonging. It is a place of inclusivity, where self-doubt is transformed into self-discovery and limitations become possibilities. Here, friendships forged in the crucible of shared experiences are not defined by ability or disability, but by the authenticity of connection. It is a testament to the fact that, at our core, we are all beautifully and wonderfully made in God's image.

It is my sincere hope that these stories inspire you to view the world through a lens of compassion and appreciation for the remarkable diversity that surrounds us. Wherever our paths may take us from here, I hope that we will all continue to be advocates for inclusivity, champions of empathy, and torchbearers of understanding. Let us always have a passion for change, growth, and the creation of a world where everyone is celebrated for who they are.

Over the past thirty years, we have learned that every person has a distinct perspective and a valuable role to play in our goal of changing lives through disability ministry. We would love to invite you to join us in that mission. And should your path ever lead you to our corner of Missouri, we would be honored to have you join us in what God is doing here. You are always welcome at Barnabas.

With kind regards,

John D. Tillack, CEO

Appendix:
A Brief History of Camp Barnabas and Barnabas Prep

1991: Paul and Cyndy Teas move from Dallas, Texas, to Branson, Missouri, where Cyndy becomes the director of nursing at Kanakuk Kamps.

1992: Cyndy learns that Lauren, a young Kanakuk camper she has become friends with, has been diagnosed with cancer and will need to have part of her leg amputated.

1993: Cyndy feels called to start a camp for kids with chronic illnesses and disabilities after a poignant conversation with Lauren.

1994: Paul and Cyndy Teas host Kanakuk Barnabas-One (KB-1)—a week of camp hosted at Kanakuk Kamps at the end of Kanakuk's regular season—for thirty-five kids with cancer and blood diseases.

1995: Paul and Cyndy host another week of camp at Kanakuk—Kanakuk Barnabas-Two (KB-2).

1996: Paul and Cyndy establish Camp Barnabas and purchase Camp Soaring Hawk, a one-hundred-plus acre camp in Purdy, Missouri. They host the first full summer of Camp Barnabas.

1998: Camp Barnabas's first Medical Center is built.

1999: Youth Specialties creates a free marketing video for Camp Barnabas, which attracts dozens of new youth groups as volunteers.

2000: Camp Barnabas's new dining hall is built.

2002: A 250,000-gallon zero-entry pool is built.

2005: Camp Barnabas is featured on ABC's *Extreme Makeover: Home Edition*. In addition to a new home for the Teas family, the team completes the Silver Lining, a recreational building for Campers; the Barnabunk, a building capable of housing forty volunteers; an eighth of a mile of new pavement through Camp; and an extensive network of underground utilities, including sewer, water, and electric. The episode later wins an Emmy.

2008: Twenty-one accessible cabins are built.

2011: Barnabas Prep is established, and six Students attend the first year's program, which is hosted at Camp Barnabas at Teas Trail in Purdy, Missouri.

2014: The property for Barnabas Prep is purchased, thanks to Gary and Norma Smalley, and Barnabas Prep moves to Branson.

2017: Professional baseball player Cole Hamels and wife, Heidi, donate a 32,000-square-foot home on Table Rock Lake, which later becomes Camp's second location: Barnabas on the Lake.

2018: Barnabas purchases the property next to Barnabas Prep's main property in Branson in order to expand Prep's program with two designated Student houses, Intern cabins, office space, classrooms, and a dining hall.

2021: A new lake is built at Camp Barnabas at Teas Trail.

2022: Barnabas Prep welcomes its largest class yet with thirty students and opens The Bears Den, a building that provides two additional classrooms, a fitness room, and a multifunctional space that's used daily.

2023: A new 10,000-square-foot, completely ADA accessible water park is constructed at Camp, featuring a lazy river, sensory zones, splash pads, and adaptive slides.

2024: Camp Barnabas celebrates its 30th anniversary.

Index of Terms:

Apostles Program: a three-week program for Missionaries seeking additional leadership training and service beyond one week at Camp

Barnabas Prep: a collegiate program in Branson, Missouri, designed to equip young adults with disabilities to achieve high levels of independence; established in 2011, Barnabas Prep is a sister ministry to Camp Barnabas

Barnabas at Teas Trail: the primary location for Camp Barnabas, located in Purdy, Missouri

Barnabas on the Lake: a second location of Camp Barnabas, located near Table Rock Lake in Shell Knob, Missouri, that was sold in 2020

Barnabreak: a weekend retreat in the fall and spring that provides a shortened version of Camp Barnabas

Barnabunk: a bunkhouse that can house up to forty volunteers at Camp; built during *Extreme Makeover: Home Edition* in 2005

Barnstormer: younger students (ages 13-14) who serve at Camp by serving food in the dining hall and tidying up around cabins

Cabin Parents: adults (ages 29+) who provide support and guidance to younger Staff and Missionaries during a week at Camp

Cabin Staff: Summer Staff employees (ages 19+) assigned to one cabin for a week at Camp to lead devotionals and support and guide Missionaries

Camp Barnabas: a summer camp for people with disabilities in Purdy, Missouri

CIA (Christians in Action): original term used for one-on-one Counselor who experiences Camp side-by-side with their Camper while caring for their needs throughout the week; this term was used from 1994 until the term Missionary replaced it

Cross Carry: a time at the end of each Camp week to remember Campers and friends of Camp who have passed away; a cross is carried to Inspiration Point and friends of the person who passed away affix a brass plaque with that person's name on it to the cross

Extreme Team: Summer Staff employees (ages 19+) who lead Camp activities such as camping excursions, the ropes course, or lifeguarding at the pool

Fellow Program: a gap year program at Barnabas Prep designed to develop young adults into Christ-like leaders who seek to serve, love, and invest in the lives of individuals with disabilities

Fellow: Barnabas Prep Staff (ages 18-23) who commits to living and serving alongside Prep Students for nine months; a Fellow lives in dorms with the Students, helps guide them through daily tasks, and invests in Students' spiritual lives, while also receiving spiritual growth and leadership training from other Staff

Inspiration Point: a bluff at the edge of Camp Barnabas's main location at Teas Trail where Campers and Missionaries go for devotions and worship services

Intern Program: a program for Barnabas Prep graduates that allows Students to live independently on campus; work at Anchor Co., an Intern-run merchandise company; find job opportunities in the Branson area and receive transportation to and from; perform volunteer work in the community; practice advanced social and life skills; and participate in Prep classes and activities, as their schedules allow

Intern: Barnabas Prep Student who has graduated from the Traditional Program and is able to live independently on campus and gain even more work and life skills while still being under Prep supervision

Missionary: one-on-one Counselor (ages 15-29) who experiences Camp side-by-side with a Camper while helping to care for their needs throughout the week

MP (Missionary Partner) Program: a former program for Campers who wanted to give back to Camp; designed for people with disabilities to serve around Camp and help support Missionaries

Rally: a midday gathering for Campers and Missionaries

Sibling "Sib" Program: a program that allows Siblings of children with disabilities to attend Camp; Siblings stay in their own cabins and have their own Cabin Counselors

The Silver Lining: a recreational building at Camp where Campers can play games; built during *Extreme Makeover: Home Edition* in 2005

Well House: Camp Barnabas's medical clinic

Wrap Up: an end-of-day gathering for all Campers and Missionaries

The Barnabas Foundation

Based in southwest Missouri, Barnabas Foundation Inc. is a nonprofit charitable organization dedicated to providing life-changing, Christ-centered experiences to individuals with disabilities and chronic illnesses. Over the past thirty years, the foundation has served more than 90,000 Campers, Missionaries, Students, and Fellows. The foundation's mission is to impact lives through disability ministry by offering opportunities to all individuals, regardless of their disability or diagnosis, and to the people who serve them by providing experiences that increase spiritual knowledge, social learning, and human dignity. To give, volunteer, or learn more, visit **campbarnabas.org** and **barnabasprep.org**.

Ruthie Burrell is the owner of Rooted Biography, LLC, a company designed to help families and ministries share their stories. She is the author of more than 140 published articles and believes in the power of stories to soften hearts, inspire people to hope and action, and reveal truth in new and unexpected ways. Ruthie lives in the Kansas City area where she enjoys exploring coffee shops or bookstores, trying out new recipes, and adventuring with her husky mix, Hugo.

www.ingramcontent.com/pod-product-compliance
Lightning Source LLC
Chambersburg PA
CBHW051623010526
44119CB00040B/487/J